"*Gone Forever But Not Forgotten* is a dynamic documentation of the good old African Safari days of yore. Rodger was smart enough to film and record his family's adventures for posterity and to share with all who will never be able to witness and revel in Old Africa again. Though the overall safari business there is thriving like never before, those old fashioned foot and tent safari days are gone forever. I know, for I was blessed to experience this spirited dynamo for myself in the wilds of Sudan back in 1978. The air, sights, sounds, smells, the mesmerizing diverse wildlife, aboriginal peoples and lifestyle, those God given sunrises and sunsets with the smell of indigenous wood smoke permeating life itself; Rodger has captured it all here and it would be a wonderful upgrade for modern people who study and learn from."

- TED NUGENT

"Rodger, your book reminds me of stories Dad told me about his safari with Derrick Dunn and brings back memories of the numerous safaris I have taken. Great job!"

- JOE JONAS, JR.

"Rodger's nostalgic *Gone Forever But Not Forgotten* is a delightful African memoir about his hunting safaris in Tanzania. Professional hunter Derrick Dunn and his famous Nyasaland tracker, Soko, are with Rodger on the dusty trail of the Big Five. In Rodger's Africa there is adventures, humor, camaraderie, and the odd medicinal sundowner that tastes pretty good after facing a charging rhino in thick stuff."

- BRIAN HERNE

"This book and DVD remind [...] early 1960's with Derrick in [...] think you hit a home run Rodger with the bases loaded."

- STAN "THE MAN" MUSIAL

"I am honored to comment on *Gone Forever But Not Forgotten* and I warmly endorse and commend Rodger's book along with its DVD on the good old days of Safari in Eastern Africa written by a devout hunter conservationist. One can never adequately write down ones comments or thoughts about a book like this, but I can honestly recommend Rodger's book as being a "great read" for anyone who is interested in the outdoors or being a hunter/ conservationist or even to the ordinary layman. Rodger's stories are "down to earth", interesting and well written, relating true stories as they actually happened, with Bwana Derrick and his faithful tracker Soko. As one reads about the Zimmerman's Safaris, one realizes why they have lasting memories of sharing campfires under the stars with Derrick, who in my opinion was one of the finest, most experienced professional hunters known to Africa."

- ERIC BALSON

"Rodger has captured the essence of Mkomazi and the magnificence of Tanzania's wonderful wilderness. His African hunting adventures have infected his passion for wildlife and its conservation. His memories will rekindle many of our own, and excite those not yet realized."

- J. BARRY TURNER

Gone Forever but Not Forgotten

Gone Forever ^{but} Not Forgotten

Rodger M. Zimmerman

A Safari Adventure

Gone Forever but Not Forgotten
A Safari Adventure

Manufactured in China

For information, please contact:
Brown Books Publishing Group
16200 North Dallas Parkway, Suite 170
Dallas, Texas 75248
www.brownbooks.com
972-381-0009
A New Era in Publishing™

ISBN-13: 978-1-933285-74-0
ISBN-10: 1-933285-74-5
LCCN 2006909575
1 2 3 4 5 6 7 8 9 10

Dedication

For Louise

Table of Contents

Acknowledgements

Louise and I wish to thank the following people: Mr. Joe Jonas Jr. for his taxidermy skills performed in the 1960s; Mr. Earl Griffith (deceased) and his son, Mr. David Griffith, for their taxidermy skills in their studios—Highland Lakes Taxidermy, Marble Falls, Texas, in the 1970s. Most of all, we thank Derrick and Heidi Dunn, without whom one of the most memorable experiences in our lives would not have been possible. They both are indeed remarkable people we love very much. Memories such as these are truly among life's greatest treasures. My thanks also goes to Ms. Pat Apple, Heidi Dunn, and Steve Stainkamp, for their talented editing, which made the book more polished. I wish to thank Ms. Blake Landfried of Dub-L-Tape, Inc. in Waco for the artwork and production of the DVD. And finally, thanks to our publisher, Brown Books Publishing Group, for their hard work and dedication.

Introduction

Neither you nor I can personally testify to what an East African safari was like at the beginning of the twentieth century. We can only read about them; no one living can describe such an experience firsthand.

At the end of World War II, with the advent of the four-wheel drive vehicle and commercial air travel, hunting safaris in East Africa quickly grew in popularity.

Technology made it faster and more convenient to travel to the continent. And it was less troublesome to access remote areas rich in wild game—incredibly vast tracts of unspoiled, virgin territory unknown to the modern boot.

Still, the convenience of getting there did little to change safari. To the chagrin of many, that would come later. For those blessed few, lucky to have been there *then*, at the pinnacle of the "golden age"—the

1950s, '60s, and to a lesser extent, the early '70s—safari was a wild and primitive immersion into a world of the untamed.

These sojourns into "the bush" could last for weeks or months (not just days) and represented a wonderfully wild baptism into the unreal—an uncut collage of encounters with native peoples, exotic, wild game, and rich, colorful landscapes. Safari meant leaving civilization behind and living in the bush, packed with everything needed to survive.

Chances were, you would not see another white man, airplane (much less a contrail), telephone line, cigarette butt, aluminum can, or bottle. You slept in canvas tents and ate wild game that you killed. Forget about television or telephones. For the first time in your humble existence, you "lived life to the fullest," witness to God's magnificent, wild creation.

The popularity of safari and the ease with which adventurers could experience it grew exponentially. Literary greats like Hemingway, Ruark, and Capstick forever seared its images into our collective consciousness.

Alas, those times are "gone forever but not forgotten."

Game animals were not on an endangered species list. But there was a conservation program initiated by the British protecting the animals from poachers, unscrupulous dictators, and corrupt politicians. There were game laws, and those who violated them were caught and punished.

The institution of game conservation programs has proven time and again to be an effective means of conservation and population growth among endangered species. At the turn of the twentieth century, few white-tailed deer remained in the State of Texas. It was only after the state began its game conservation program that the whitetail rallied. Today, the Texas Parks and Wildlife Department has to plead with licensed hunters to take their limit because in certain areas, deer are so plentiful that they can starve due to overgrazing.

The polar bear is another example of sound game conservation. Due to scientific programs and strict management, the polar bear has prospered. It's the same with the Bengal tiger, pulled back from the brink of extinction by resolute action and strict conservation measures.

In the late 1950s, the British surveyed black rhino populations in East Africa and concluded that there were some twenty-seven thousand animals remaining. That was before the independence of Uganda, Kenya, and Tanganyika (aka, Tanzania).

Today, *wild* black rhino are all but gone, poached out for their "horn," the distinctive, tightly woven, double-hair protuberance on this magnificent animal's snout.

In many places, the elephant has fared almost as badly. Poaching remains rampant for both the black rhino and the elephant. There are laws to punish poachers, but there is little to no will to enforce such laws, and at best, there is ineffective or no punishment for offenders.

Lawfully regulated hunting has not brought about the demise of any wild animal in North America or Africa. For those who believe regulated, lawful hunting is the cause of animal extinction, with due respect, you are woefully ill informed.

Preface

hat follows is a first-hand account of eighty-one glorious hunting days spent in Tanzania, East Africa, during the late 1960s and early 1970s. It is a true story, an adventure taken by myself and my wife, Louise, who has been my best hunting companion and a wonderful, loving wife, without whom my life would not have been complete.

Louise and I have hunted together in Africa, India, Alaska, British Columbia, other parts of Canada, New Zealand, and most all of the central and western United States, including Texas, our home. She is an excellent long-gun shot and a true sportswoman-conservationist.

For those of you fortunate to have experienced safari during the 1950s into the mid-1970s with a *genuine* professional hunter (PH) at your side, the following chronicle will no doubt evoke strong memories. For those of you who have not known the experience of safari, this story is intended to describe what it used to be like, but alas, is no longer.

Today's safari, in my opinion, is not at all like safaris of old. *Webster's* defines safari as, "a journey or hunting expedition in East Africa or a caravan of such an expedition."

In two of the three East African countries, Uganda and Kenya, hunting is no longer allowed. Tanzania remains the last vestige of East African safari hunting.

Today's experience is an abbreviated version of yesteryear's, more a "fly in" or "drive in" abbreviated trip to an established lodge, touting all the twenty-first century amenities. Today's safari hunter does not experience the bush in all its vast splendor, with all its vast herds of wild animals. That said, today's professional hunters are a shadow of those who preceded them, proudly blazing a trail across that vast, inhospitable landscape. Today, sadly, far too many are motivated more by the dollar than their love of safari and Africa's wild places and wild things.

This, of course, is one man's opinion—mine. There may be those who disagree; they can write their own book.

Having traveled life's highway these seventy-one years, I have reached the mountain peak; I am on the downhill slide. I'm in good health, and I do most of the things I once did, albeit slower and not as well.

I can't complain. My life has been grand! I've had a

most successful criminal defense practice for forty-five years without ever having a grievance filed against me. Of that fact, I'm quite proud.

I was blessed with wonderful parents and lucky to be born and raised in a small Texas town. As I grew, the outdoors and hunting became integral parts of my life. My father gave me my first rifle, a Remington single-shot, bolt-action .22, when I was seven and taught me how to safely use it.

The years passed and a tour in the United States Army and law school were completed. I began to practice law, which left me little time for fishing and hunting. But I gradually became a bit more organized in my practice, and I felt the irresistible lure—the call of the

Dark Continent and the African "Big Five" (i.e., lion, leopard, elephant, buffalo, and rhino).

I learned of a hunting organization—Game Conservation International—that met each odd year in San Antonio, Texas. Louise and I joined Game Coin, as it was called, and attended the organization's convention in May 1969. It was there that we met Mr. and Mrs. Derrick Dunn. Derrick was a well-known East African PH who lived in Arusha, Tanzania, with his charming wife, Heidi.

Prior to attending Game Coin's convention, I'd heard of Derrick from a taxidermist friend in Houston, Earl Griffith, and another friend, Dr. John Mike McCullough, in Corpus Christi. The men had hunted with Derrick in Tanzania several times. (We were recently saddened by the news of Earl's passing.)

As a consequence of my friends' favorable hunting experiences and references, I visited with Derrick at the convention, where I booked a thirty-day Tanzanian safari for July 1969.

I don't recommend booking a hunt with a professional hunter—regardless of where or what you plan to hunt—without meeting him first or at least speaking with others who have hunted with him. Too many things can happen if you don't first investigate a PH, and most of them are bad.

You certainly wouldn't hunt with a professional hunter who couldn't hit the side of a barn with a shot-gun, especially when you intend to hunt dangerous game—lest we forget, he's your only backup. Such animals can kill you, and some will eat you whether you are dead or alive.

In conversation, I learned that Derrick was born in England and moved to Africa in 1946 at the age of twenty. He became a professional hunter in the early 1950s, and the rest, as they say, is history. Derrick and I became strong and fast friends, and we inked a deal with a handshake. I was ready to go.

After the convention, Louise and I returned home, where we had a heart-to-heart talk about my safari purchase, whereupon she informed me that it might be best if I went alone. During my absence, she would care for our eight-year-old son, Michael. I concurred, although I would have preferred she go with me. All the while, something deep inside me (some sixth sense or primordial urge) told me one safari would never be enough and that I would return again to Africa—and I had yet to make my first trip!

During a visit to my dad's home in San Marcos, Texas, where my law office was located, I told him of my scheduled trip to Tanzania. Dad was extremely pleased and said that he had always wanted to go, but at age seventy-six, he was no longer up for it. Dad surprised me when he suggested I take my brother. "If Frank can go," he said, "I'll pay for the safari."

Frank was a colonel in the United States Air Force, and he was able to take off the entire month of July.

Without hesitation, Frank agreed and our great adventure had begun.

CHAPTER ONE

Getting Ready

A lot more of Africa gets into your blood than the malaria, you know.

—Peter Hathaway Capstick, *Death in the Long Grass*, 1977

lanning a safari—then or now—is a serious and expensive proposition. For those interested in going, I recommend considering several factors that are integral to a successful safari.

First, and most importantly, get to know your professional hunter. After you have met with your PH or spoken to others who can vouch for his trustworthiness, professionalism, and reliability, it is left for you to finalize the deal and make the arrangements (e.g., contract signing, airfare, and passport).

Clothing—Study your destination of choice and the climate at the precise time of year you plan to visit. Keep in mind: Africa's seasons are the reverse of ours here on the North American continent. Winters in the southern hemisphere are the reverse of ours—our winter is their summer and vice versa.

Proper clothing—and a good hat—are critical when preparing for safari. There are no stores in the middle of the bush, and finding ordinary items such as shirts, pants, and socks is all but impossible.

In Africa's cities—or in the field—you can't rely on anyone but yourself to supply all of your basic needs. Sitting in a leopard blind in the dark, with a crescent moon shining overhead and the noises of the African bush echoing in your ears, can be a bone-chilling experience—in terms of nerves as well as ambient temperature. Be prepared and do your homework.

Trophies—You should have an idea of the species you hope to garner. Speak with your professional hunter to glean which animals are likely to be found where you will be hunting. And remember, that's why it's called hunting—not killing. You may or may not be fortunate enough to find and actually bag the animals you want to hang on your wall.

Chances are, though, your hunt will be successful. Assuming you have chosen a reputable PH, he is more than qualified to put you on the species you seek. Still, it's hunting and many variables can and often do interfere with one's safari success.

Be certain to ask your PH which animals you can take and what trophy fees apply. Not only must a hunter pay for his hunt; he must also pay a trophy fee for each animal. And that does not include dressing the animal and having the carcass professionally processed prior to being returned to the United States so that your taxidermist may do his work.

Determine if your animal requires a CITES permit to be legally brought back into the United States. Check with the United States Fish and Wildlife Department before ever booking your African safari.

Weapons—Knowing what you intend to hunt should indicate what firearm you should use. Every hunter has his or her firearm preference. I have hunted in Africa five times, and I will tell you, African game is the hardiest found anywhere on the planet.

If I could possess one firearm to hunt any creature on earth, and feel confident doing so, it would be a Winchester Model 70, .375 H&H Magnum. For thin-skinned animals, I would use a 270-grain, soft-point bullet; for thick-skinned animals, I would use a 300-grain, solid-metal-case bullet.

Many big-game safari hunters and professional hunters prefer the big magnums—the .458 and the .470. Others have comfortably and successfully used the .30.06 and the .270 for plains game.

Take your firearm to a U.S. Customs office for the proper certification before departing. Without this paperwork, you will not be able to return your weapons to the United States. Check with your airline to determine the proper handling of your weapon and its ammunition.

Bullet Placement—Forget everything you may have heard about behind-the-shoulder shot placement for North American game. The only "sweet spot" on African species is the shoulder—*period*. Contrary to what others may say, this is especially true for the elephant, which I will discuss later.

Regardless of firearm or bullet choice, for your own safety and that of your fellow hunters, be absolutely certain that your rifle shoots well and that you are fully capable of hitting your target—BEFORE YOU EVER LEAVE HOME. More will be said later about this.

Inoculations—Consult your physician and the Center for Disease Control and Prevention (CDC) well before leaving.

Medication—It goes without saying, if you require prescribed medication, bring an ample supply. Although your PH may be adequately supplied with medications, it is not a bad idea to speak with your family physician and get a prescription for antibiotics to take along.

Have your physician prescribe a strong pain medication in the event you need it. And you should certainly advise your professional hunter of any foods to which you may be allergic.

Creature Comforts—It is unlikely your favorite soft drink, alcohol, or smoke will be available in Africa. Plan accordingly.

Trip Record—Finally, I advise taking a decent digital video camera with sound. Without a doubt, safari will be one of the greatest experiences of your life. Record it for posterity—you'll be glad you did.

CHAPTER TWO

Longido

 1969

The free, self-reliant, adventurous life, with its rugged and stalwart democracy; the wild surroundings, the grand beauty of the scenery, the chance to study the ways and habits of the woodland creatures—all these unite to give to the career of the wilderness hunter its peculiar charm.

—Teddy Roosevelt, *The Wilderness Hunter*, 1893

e prepared for twelve different inoculations that were required for contagious diseases (e.g., bubonic plague, yellow fever, typhus, typhoid, etc.). I was fortunate to have big brother Frank along, as he was a medical doctor and provided ample advice for our added comfort and protection.

As neither Frank nor I had previously been on safari, we discussed firearm choices, my forte. I agreed that I would take my .30.06 and .458 rifles. Frank brought a .300 Magnum.

I arranged the schedule with Derrick and advised Frank. We agreed to meet in New York for the transatlantic flight to Africa aboard a TWA DC Stretch-8 jet with a pair of engines mounted on either wing.

To illustrate the stark contrast between yesteryear and today's air travel, an unfortunate victim of 9/11, I was allowed to carry both rifles on the plane as carry-on luggage. As I ascended the roll-away steps leading up to the fuselage, the pilot engaged me in friendly banter about my weapons.

"Going hunting?" he asked.

"I sure am," I replied.

"Where ya' headed?"

"Africa," I shot back.

As it turned out, the pilot was a hunting enthusiast who had ventured to Alaska to hunt North American big game. He was especially interested in the .458, which I removed from its case as he admired the weapon—in the cockpit of the aircraft. You won't see that in today's world.

"What kind of load does this bad boy shoot?" he quizzed.

"Shoots a 500-grain solid," I said. "Should be hell on elephants."

The captain whistled and responded saying, "Good luck."

Frank and I flew from New York to Nairobi on June 30, 1969. Upon arriving, Derrick dutifully collected us at the airport and drove us to his country home in Arusha, Tanzania.

When we arrived, we were informed that Derrick's crew, simply referred to as "the boys," had already set up our first base camp in the bush two hours away in Longido. Longido is northeast of Arusha, near the Tanzanian-Kenyan border in the scenic foothills of Mount Kilimanjaro. As expected, the boys had the camp glistening when we arrived.

When Frank and I first saw that setting, we were blown away, immediately reminded of Hollywood director Henry King's blockbuster movie, *The Snows of Kilimanjaro*, starring Gregory Peck. The view in that 1952 flick was just as breathtaking and spectacular as it was in person in 1969. Indeed, our tents may well have been located under the same overarching acacias as the ones moviegoers marveled at in the movie. Had starlets Ava Gardner and Susan Hayward trod the same soil?

Frank stepped forward. "Give me the damn thing," he swaggered. "I'll show you guys how it's done."

Frank missed the tree entirely. We checked the scope, and upon closer inspection, the scope mounts wiggled at the slightest touch. I put the .30.06 rifle aside and forgot it.

After that fiasco, we moved through the bush looking for game. Everywhere we looked, the bush came alive with plains game. There were ample numbers of impala, Thompson's gazelle, and zebra, several of which we took that first day and all of which are antelopes. There were also warthogs and diminutive versions of the Big Five—too small to shoot.

Plains game include impala, steinbok, eland, bushbuck, reedbuck, topi, (the long-necked) gerenuk, waterbuck, steinbok, and dik-dik. All are delicious table fare, and when one was shot, nothing was wasted. What we didn't eat in camp, the boys ate. And what they didn't eat, they took home.

Derrick's crew consisted of ten natives, each with two or more wives and numerous children at home. For the boys, safari represented a lucrative job and a much-needed source of protein for their families.

Soko and Mageli spotted a large herd of Cape buffalo (*mbogo* in Swahili), and the hunt was on. Mbogo is one of the Big Five, and as a result of our agreement, Frank was first to shoot, assuming we were to locate a worthy trophy.

Derrick made a few attempts to spot a bull, but the herd kept moving. We followed the buffalo quite a way before they slowed enough for Derrick to spot a good bull.

At that time, a fifty-inch bull was an extra-fine trophy. Anything in the mid- to high-forty-inch range was considered a good bull.

Everyone exited the vehicle and started out after the herd in the thick, Tanzanian brush. We had cover, and the wind was right; conditions were favorable.

Derrick carried his .470 double Rigby, Frank wielded his .300 Magnum, and I had a Super 8 camera (cutting-edge technology, at the time, with no sound). Soko and Mageli traipsed behind us.

As we crept through the bush, leapfrogging from one bush to the next and drawing closer to the game,

I could tell Derrick was apprehensive about Frank's shooting system. It was not the caliber Derrick objected to as much as Frank's bullet choice.

Earlier, a gunsmith in the States had rechambered my brother's rifle to accommodate a Weatherby load. There was nothing wrong with that. But Frank had loaded 200- or 300-grain bullets, insisting that with the proper shot placement, the soft-nosed bullets would do a j-o-b on a big Cape buffalo. It was Frank's contention that such a load would penetrate the tough hide of Mbogo, pierce the fierce beast's heart, and drop him in his tracks. That was the plan.

Sympathetic to Derrick's fears, I insisted Frank try my pre-'64, Model 70 Winchester in .458 Magnum; my brother declined the offer.

Frank is a more technical firearms man than I. He reloads his own ammunition, and he can tell you all about foot pounds of energy at the muzzle of the rifle, foot seconds the bullet will travel at any distance, and weight of the bullet.

Back to our story. We stalked that big bull to within forty-five yards. He stood with his left flank toward us, looking at us askance with a snarl. Frank is a decent shot—I'll give him that—but his choice of ammo was inadequate.

My brother slammed a round into a spot directly behind the great beast's left shoulder. The bull went down with a thud, flat on his stomach, as though all four legs had sunk into quicksand up to the animal's midsection.

Far from dead, the buffalo growled, bellowed, and sprang to his feet as quickly as he had collapsed. Luckily, he charged away from us.

My only weapon was the Super 8. I steadied the movie camera, all the while trying to keep the bull centered in the viewfinder. As a result, I didn't see how Frank performed immediately after his first shot.

I heard Derrick yell, "Shoot him again! Shoot him again!" Frank hesitated.

I heard my brother eject the spent round, and I heard him as he chambered another into the bolt-action rifle. Frank touched off a second shot, which I later learned struck the bull on the rump. I did not see the round hit, but I could not miss the unmistakable *whop* when it struck flesh.

Still, the bull remained on his feet, tearing through brush to escape. By this time, the wounded beast was very sick, although still moving at a clip. At that juncture, Derrick handed Frank his .470 Rigby.

Derrick wrested Frank's .300 Magnum from my brother's hands and in words too strong to mistake, yelled, "Shoot him with this!"

Frank brought down the buff with one shot to the back of the head. My brother was amazed that the bull had been so tough.

As we approached the animal, Frank asked Derrick to have the boys excise his round to determine where the first slug had wound up inside the bull's chest cavity. To Frank's dismay, his shot had penetrated the tough hide and lodged a mere six inches inside, never reaching the heart. Frank admitted our PH had been right; his loads were far from adequate.

We spent a number of days taking non-Big-Five species such as the dik-dik (the smallest of Africa's antelope), eland, impala, bushbuck, warthog, reedbuck, topi, and gerenuk. We filled the rest of our field time hunting African sandgrouse and yellow-necked francolin—both delectable table fare.

Ten days into hunting Longido, Soko spotted rhino tracks as we were making our way through the bush, and Derrick stopped the vehicle to have a closer look. Without a doubt, the tracks had been made by a large, male black rhino. It was my turn for the Big Five, and Derrick sealed the deal by affirming, "Let's track this bad boy and see what he looks like."

My .458 Winchester was loaded with 500-grain solids, my choice for rhino. Derrick concurred, as the rhino is as tough as or tougher than the buffalo.

Soko was Derrick's number one tracker; the two had been together since Derrick first became a professional hunter. Soko knew his business.

As we followed the tracks, Soko paused now and then to observe small bushes along the trail. He confirmed to Derrick that the tracks had indeed been made by a male rhino. Soko added that the rhino had stopped to browse on the bush that he was now hidden behind not twenty minutes earlier.

When Derrick translated the conversation to me, I was incredulous. "Come on, Derrick," I said. "Be serious. Soko can tell that rhino ate on this bush twenty minutes ago?"

"You better believe he can!" Derrick replied. I wasn't convinced, but I was encouraged.

We had the wind in our face, which was a distinct advantage, as a rhino's sense of smell is well above average in the animal world. And according to our PH, there's nothing wrong with a rhino's eyesight either.

We had gone half a mile when we saw the rhino standing broadside to us, his left side in clear view.

I had a four-power, rifle scope on my .458, the effective range of which is only seventy to eighty yards with a 500-grain solid bullet. The rhino hadn't spotted us, so I took my time getting a good sight picture. I secured a solid rest, took a deep breath, and squeezed the trigger.

The .458 Magnum packs a wallop—on both ends. Before my feet touched back to earth, the rhino had cut right, and off he went. He stopped behind very thick cover before I could take another shot. Derrick couldn't believe it. Excited as he was, he could only say, "You shot too low."

After I caught my breath, I responded, "The hell you say, Derrick. You're full of it. I hit that rascal right in the middle of the neck, and it should have broken his neck."

It was then that I realized why my professional hunter had repeated his mantra nonstop since the outset: "Everything in Africa demands a high shoulder shot to penetrate the chest cavity and break the shoulder."

What troubled me was that we had only one rhino permit for this safari, only one of two permits issued by the Game Department that year. Each rhino permit cost over eleven hundred U.S. dollars, and it mattered not if you wounded and failed to recover your rhino. The cost was the same. You had but one chance, and wounding an animal was not in my game plan.

I told Derrick I didn't care how far we walked or how long it took; we were not going to lose that rhino. I owed it to the animal, and besides, I had a place reserved for that hulking brute in my trophy room in Texas.

Unfortunately, my rhino was headed downwind of our position, and that meant he could not miss picking up our scent as we tracked him. As we followed, we could see from the tracks that the animal was indeed very sick. "If he is not dead yet, he will probably lie down," Derrick said.

We tracked that big fellow for the better part of a mile when Soko stopped dead in his tracks. Our tracker turned and told Derrick that the rhino was ahead, lying down.

Derrick turned and said with all the intensity he could muster, "Rodger, he's probably going to charge if he has anything left. Get ready."

We stood there frozen in time, waiting to see what would happen. The wind was at our back—not a good thing. I had my .458 at ready arms, and Derrick peered over the muzzle of his powerful .470 as spouts of dust blew skyward from the rhino's flared nostrils. Derrick spoke through clenched lips, "Don't shoot till I say so."

Derrick exhaled audibly. "Aim between the eyes," he insisted. "If he presents a shoulder shot, take it."

My pulse quickened, my breath grew short and spasmodic. Questions flew through my brain: *Would*

I make a good shot? Could I stand up to a wounded rhino's charge? Was I really ready?

Sweat beaded on my brow. I wiped my sweaty palm on my pants and resumed my rifle grip.

The scene played out in slow motion as the rhino started his charge. My heart pounded so hard I felt sure it would burst from my chest.

I knew the sound of my heart beating was audible to Derrick, certainly to the boys—most certainly to the wounded rhino. The rhino started toward us, head down. He approached with stumbling gait; I waited for the command. Derrick screamed, "Shoot!"

The rhino slowed twenty yards out, made a slight turn to his left, and exposed the right flank. I drew down and fired. Before I could reload and fire a second salvo, Derrick fired twice in rapid succession. I heard both shots strike. The beast ran forty feet to our right and collapsed in a heap.

My shirt was soaked. My hands trembled. We approached the animal, and I could see the spot where my first round had struck the rhino's swollen neck. But because he had collapsed on his right side, I could not see the shot I had made as the rhino charged us. Derrick's two shots to the rhino's right side were obscured as well.

It took four of us to roll that monster over to examine the shot placement. It was not an easy job—Derrick estimated the animal's weight at just over a ton.

When we finally got the rhino turned and inspected, one round had struck him in the rib cage and the other in the belly. The shot that I was so concerned about had struck his right shoulder, exactly where I had aimed.

I was happy about my shot placement, and Derrick complimented me. After that incident, my PH never questioned my ability to handle myself under pressure or shoot a rifle at a dangerous, charging animal.

My first Big-Five trophy was a black rhino with a "horn" that measured seventeen inches in length. At that time, this was an "acceptable" trophy; animals sporting twenty inches or more were deemed exceptional in the day when they could be hunted.

17" black rhino

Black rhino no longer exist in the wild. There are pockets of this statuesque creature in guarded enclosures—a step above zoo status. But for all intents and purposes, the great beasts are all but gone from their range.

Note: the black rhino's demise was not a result of "lawful" hunting; rather it was a result of poaching. Today, one does not venture to Africa to hunt the Big Five, as the black rhino is gone forever but not forgotten. Today's hunts are termed the "Big Four." And only in Tanzania can the Big Four—lion, leopard, elephant, and buffalo—be legally hunted.

I shot my black rhino on July 20, 1969. That date will no doubt ring a bell with historians reading this account. Indeed, many of my readers were not born then or are too young to remember. But July 20, 1969, represents a special anniversary for me and many of my fellow Americans.

We sat around the fireplace that evening, enjoying our first toasty (cocktail), gawking at a brilliant East African full moon. Nights in Africa are very special.

We had no telephone or any form of outside communication, save a wireless radio. A day or two earlier, sitting around the campfire, we had received a radio transmission from a Nairobi station reporting that American astronaut and Apollo 11 Commander Neil Armstrong would soon embark on a historic moon landing.

On July 20, 1969, Commander Neil Armstrong became the first man to land a craft on the moon and the first to step on the moon's surface.

I asked Derrick to call the boys together, all ten of them, to join us at fireside. Derrick was curious. "What is it you want?" he asked.

"Just call them here, please," I insisted.

Derrick gathered the boys, and I asked him to relay to them that at that very moment, there was an American flying about in his airplane and that he traveled all the way from the earth to the moon for the first time.

I'll never forget Derrick's response: "Bully, frightfully ripping *what*! Good idea, Rodger."

There was a bit of Swahili exchanged, and Derrick smiled broadly. I waited anxiously for his reply—their reaction. The boys' expressions were deadpan.

"Well, they really don't think much about it," Derrick reported.

I was aghast. "Why not?" I moaned.

Derrick made a grand sweep with his arms. He gestured from one horizon to the next. "Because every once in a great while, they see white men fly their airplanes from there to there, and if man can accomplish that, what difference does it make if he is able to fly from here to there?" Derrick pointed first to the earth and then to the bright moon above. "After all, old chap," he concluded, "it's much closer." That childlike, simplistic African logic astounds me to this day.

That night, the sky in the southern hemisphere was blanketed with a myriad of stars. The Southern Cross was clearly discernible, and it was my first time to ever see it. There were so many stars in that black velvet sky, it was impossible to imagine room for any more. The firmament resembled a calm lake at sunset with a light rain sparkling on its surface.

The temperature that early evening was near fifty degrees Fahrenheit, making our campfire time before dinner a real pleasure.

As we sat around the blazing logs, embers crackling and scarlet sparks rising to heaven, we enjoyed our toasties and Asmani's tasty *samosas* (little meat-filled, flour-roll snacks packed with spicy, ground antelope meat).

We relived every minute of the day's hunt and the retrieval of my black rhino trophy. The conversation gravitated to the moon landing, and we hoped all was going well for the American astronauts.

We had one more day to hunt Longido before leaving for our next adventure, the Maswa hunting area on the Serengeti Plain—a two-day drive from Arusha.

The next morning, we traveled for miles into extremely thick bush, where we came upon the tracks of two rather large bull elephants. We stopped the vehicle, got our tracking gear together, and moved out to follow the tracks.

Soko was leading; Derrick trailed behind him. Frank was behind Derrick because it was his turn at one of the Big Five. This time, my brother wisely accepted the .458 I offered him to hunt elephant.

The vegetation was very thick, and the ground was covered in what Derrick called "wait-a-bit bush." This African plant species derives its common name from the entanglement one experiences when trapped in the thorny stuff. Literally, you become ensnared, forced to "wait a bit" before extricating yourself and moving on.

We walked through that thicket for what seemed

like an hour. As we moved, we stopped frequently to check the tracks and the wind. If you can avoid being detected by an elephant, you are much better off. If an elephant "winds" you, it can either move off or become aggressive and charge. We wanted neither scenario, so we moved slowly and quietly upwind.

I was behind Frank, but Derrick—ahead of Frank—was clearly visible, as I was the number-three man in a snaking line. The first thing I noticed was that Frank had stopped. Then I saw Derrick standing in front of Frank about five feet away.

It was very quiet except for the noisy elephant, which was in front of Derrick. The great beast had his trunk and tusks raised in a tree, tearing branches off, cram-

I was very pleased with the ivory. One tusk weighed seventy-nine pounds, and the other went eighty-three pounds. Both were beautifully matched. Now I had animal number two of my Big Five. What remained of my Big Five was a leopard, a lion, and a buffalo.

Cleaning an elephant is no small task. It's time consuming, to say the least. The boys removed the ivory, skinned out the ears, and removed the tail and all four feet for the taxidermist. This process took hours.

We arrived at camp in the late afternoon and prepared to leave Longido. Tomorrow, we would travel to Maswa, on the Serengeti Plain. Longido had been a hunting experience of a lifetime, yet we were anxious to see a new area with different species and terrain.

Very early the next morning, the boys began to tear down our camp, and Derrick, Frank, and I headed to Derrick's home in Arusha, where we would meet the boys later that afternoon.

When the boys arrived, we stocked and loaded the vehicles with the necessary supplies for our next fifteen days in the bush, and we were off and away.

CHAPTER THREE

Maswa

 1969

There are several very good reasons why, despite the surprising number of man-eating incidents that occur today in Africa, most are hushed up like an epidemic of social disease at a Bible school. It's the same reason that Florida chambers of commerce don't go out of their way to spread the word of shark attacks along their beaches.

—Peter Hathaway Capstick, *Death in the Long Grass*, 1977

We drove to Lake Manyara and made our way up and around the slope of the Ngorongoro Crater to its rim. The ten-mile-wide crater features two-thousand-foot walls and is considered the eighth wonder of the world.

Lake Manyara is an hour and a half drive west of Arusha and encompasses two hundred square miles of water when the lake levels are high. The lake stretches for more than thirty miles along the Rift Valley escarpment, home to numbers of wildebeest, buffalo, hyena, lions, cheetah, leopard, jackal, and plains game.

That day we stayed the night at a beautiful lodge overlooking the floor of the crater. The crater floor was simply alive with animals. It is colossal—scientists say it is the result of a massive volcanic explosion or implosion.

The crater rim reaches skyward seven to eight thousand feet, and if you glass the flat crater floor—at elevation five thousand feet—you will see zebra, Thomson's gazelle, impala, warthogs, wildebeest, antelope, and the big cats.

Early the next morning, we started off on one of the most unbelievably beautiful drives through paradise. Derrick, Frank, Soko, Mageli, and I were in the lead Land Rover. Saidi, our driver-mechanic, followed in the second Rover.

The six-ton truck was loaded with everything we would need for the next fifteen days and was driven by one of the other boys. The rest of Derrick's hands rode in the big truck.

I would describe the Serengeti as vast, rolling plains covered in undulating grasses, with a tree here and there. It was as though you could see forever, and as you considered infinity, the animals were everywhere.

The great plain was populated with vast herds of African game. There were giraffe and zebra—contrasted with a solitary black rhino cow and her young calf—running and standing, gazing back at us. Black-backed jackals and long-legged ostriches loped along beside the vehicle. Great herds of wildebeest fed alongside antelope and mingled with spotted hyena, elephant, full-mane lions, and rhino.

Talk about sensory overload! There were far too many natural wonders for my human eyes to behold. You might spy a spotted hyena poking its head from a hole, wondering what on earth we might be. Serengeti was a teeming expanse as far as the eye could see.

The drive across the plains was not all easy going. There were many rough places to cross and multiple ditches and ravines for the vehicles to circumvent. It was the dry season, but there was water about.

The grass was green enough for that time of year, according to Derrick. To me, a Texan from the Hill Country, it looked magnificently verdant. Back in my neck of the woods, it was summertime—hot and dry, a caliche backdrop interspersed with patches of scrub cedar.

This area called Maswa was home to five hundred square miles of prime East African hunting country. Some animals found here were also common to Longido, but each area had its unique wildlife. Lions, leopards, and buffalo were common to both, and I had not bagged any in Longido.

When we reached our new campsite, we found it to be another beautiful spot to pitch our tents. This would be home—headquarters—for the next two weeks.

Nothing resembled civilization. There were no cigarette butts, cans, or bottles lying about—only pristine, wild African bush country. Indeed, I don't recall ever seeing an airplane fly over during our entire safari.

As I looked away from our Maswa camp, in any direction, there was no sign of the familiar. It could easily have been in the seventeenth, eighteenth, or nineteenth century.

The balance of the day at the new campsite was spent resting and visiting about the last two weeks' safari and the upcoming fifteen days.

After toasties and dinner, we went to bed hoping the following day, or one of the days to come, would bring us closer to another of the Big Five.

Everyone was up very early the next morning. The air was charged with a sense of expectancy. After dressing and wolfing down a hearty breakfast of eggs and meat, we loaded up the vehicles and made our way into the bush.

It's tough describing what we saw first because the Serengeti literally came alive. Animals were everywhere. Seeing them was not the problem—selecting a quality trophy and going after it was.

The first day we located a magnificent, full-mane lion. This was definitely a shooter. The King of the Jungle was an impressive beast, and since it was my turn at another of the Big Five, I decided to take him.

With my .30.06 out of commission, I had but one choice—my tried-and-true .458 Magnum. We exited the Rover and began to cover ground in the direction the lion had last been seen walking.

After several hundred yards, we saw the big guy standing beneath a spreading thorn bush, appearing as though he had just awoken. His mouth agape, the old boy uttered a soft yawn and grunted. He had not seen us nor caught our scent.

We inched closer, to forty yards, when Derrick raised his hand.

"This is close enough, Rodger. Now, shoot." The distance between us was dangerously close; a wounded lion can span that distance in a heartbeat.

Many a man has stared into a mature lion's eyes and flinched. Yet I felt confident with my marksman's skills—and my weapon of choice. I was also imminently confident in my friend, my PH, Derrick. Beads of sweat formed on my face, my arms, and my neck as I drew down on that lion and fixed my sight

Rodger's lion—mounted

pattern. I aimed at the beast's shoulder and fired. *Ka-boom!* The .458 exploded in my hands. Overhead, birds scattered in the trees.

The 510-grain soft point struck my prey squarely on the shoulder. Hit hard, the lion lurched but wilted almost instantly.

The boys piled from the trucks, and high fives rang out. We approached carefully and examined the big male to make sure he was dead. This was a beautiful trophy with a black mane heavier in the front than in the back.

The scales do not lie. My lion weighed slightly more than four hundred and fifty pounds. And with that single shot from the .458, I had bagged my third member of the Big Five.

Again, the boys did their work with the carcass, and they loaded the lion into the back of the Rover for our return to camp and a rendezvous with the skinner.

Now I only lacked a buffalo and a leopard to complete my Big Five. Otherwise, I had my sights set on various species of plains game.

I never could have imagined how tough African game is to bring down. When I spied a male ostrich trotting alongside our vehicle, I asked Derrick to stop and let me collect him for a pair of cowboy boots.

Derrick dutifully stopped, and I hit that large, feathered target smack dab on his broad shoulder with the .458, shooting a soft-nosed, 510-grain bullet. The ostrich dropped his wing but failed to go down. Only after we followed him several hundred feet did he give up the ghost.

Frank and I also collected dik-dik (one of the greatest eating animals in Africa), eland, topi, zebra, kongoni, lesser kudu, bushbuck, and steinbuck.

With those feats accomplished and only a few days remaining on safari, we decided to concentrate on the remaining Big Five.

We traveled far and hunted hard before locating a large herd of buffalo that easily numbered in the hundreds. We felt certain there had to be one fine bull in the group.

Derrick followed the herd in and around, back and forth, and through thick bush until the herd slowed, and we finally spotted a large bull. We worked ourselves into position, hoping to separate the bull from the herd.

As planned, the bull separated and lagged some distance behind. Driving very slowly, Derrick put us in a position to get out of the Rover and take a shot. I grabbed the .458 from my gun bearer; it was loaded with a lethal, 500-grain solid bullet.

I was ready to go. The bull was walking at a gait, but when he turned his head and neck, I fired.

I have heard stories where buffalo have been shot multiple times before expiring. Other stories I have heard report wounded buffalo that are never recovered. On that day, my shooting system and marksmanship sealed that great bull's fate with a single, well-placed shot. Down he went, in a heap.

Mine was one fine specimen. The buff measured forty-four inches and sported an impressive boss. He was a prime candidate for a beautiful shoulder mount in my Texas trophy room, where he hangs to this day.

To complete my hunt, there remained only the leopard, which I ultimately bagged with two days remaining on our safari.

Before we continue, let's take a look at the native people who live where I hunted.

THE MASAI

The Masai are a nomadic tribe of East Africa, indigenous to the Serengeti Plain. Masai ranch cattle and their warriors are historically known as some of the fiercest African fighters and hunters. A very hardy people, they seldom eat meat; rather, they live on a diet of mixed cow blood and milk.

They move about the grasslands, herding and grazing their cattle. And as they move from place to place, Masai build huts—*manyattas*—where they remain until their cattle have grazed the grass in that area.

Masai exist under conditions that would be appalling to westerners. Cleanliness, as we know it, doesn't exist. During the time I spent in Africa, I never once saw these proud people wash. That is not to say that with an abundance of water—a rarity—they will not wash. I just never witnessed the spectacle. The women, children, and men are covered with flies, and as a consequence, often suffer infections.

Masai boys undergo tribal circumcision at puberty—their rite of passage into the world of manhood. Should a Masai youth flinch or show fear during the painful circumcision process, he and his family are disgraced, and the boy is labeled a coward.

Once a male has reached manhood through circumcision, he is a warrior tasked with three duties: procreation, fighting, and hunting.

Women, older men, and children are responsible for

the myriad of familial responsibilities—including caring for the much-valued cattle.

A Masai warrior is a formidable hunting and fighting machine, capable of running for miles at a stretch. Their hand-crafted spears and shields are masterfully created and extremely lethal. I have several spears and shields in my personal collection, and I can tell you, the razor-sharp cutting edge of a Masai spear is perfectly balanced with a stout wooden handle—an ideal weapon for precision throwing and the spearing of game.

We encountered many Masai warriors as we traveled through the bush, and fortunately they were peaceful enough, although not always as communicative as we might have liked. Masai warriors do not like having their photographs taken, but I was able to do so with some tomfoolery.

I was amazed at how the Masai are able to herd their cattle into areas void of the infamous tsetse fly. How they do this is unknown to me, because if there is any living creature in the vicinity with blood in its veins, the tsetse will attack and drain blood immediately.

Tsetse flies are not like the horsefly that we know in the United States. A member of the housefly family, they are yellowish to brown in color with an extended proboscis that juts from their heads like a dagger.

These nasty little bloodsuckers are carriers of fatal diseases (i.e., nagana) in horses and cattle but to which African wild game seems to have developed immunities. Likewise, the tsetse can transmit sleeping sickness to humans. Tsetse flies loved me in Africa, and they seemed especially fond of the whites in our camp.

Tsetses strike their victims much like a dive-bomber, and as soon as the creature reaches its target, the blood begins to flow. The bite is extremely painful. If you slap one very hard when he lands on you, it doesn't affect him at all. If you want to kill one, you have to slap him extremely hard and grind him against your flesh. Tsetse flies seem immune to insect repellant— even those containing deet. In my experience, repellants are worthless and may even attract the flies like cheap perfume.

THE NDOROBO

The Ndorobo are the "honey hunters" of East Africa. These men are fearless human beings with an uncanny ability to climb. Ndorobo men climb trees and poke their hands into huge colonies of honeybees that could carry a man away if they decided it was in their best interest.

To watch one of those old gents rob a hive was a real backwoods hoot. How they came away without being stung all over their bodies was a remarkable feat and yet another great African mystery.

In the last ten years, the American press has sounded the alarm from coast to coast, raising a hue and cry about "killer bees amongst us." Yet little do most

Americans know, the bees that are causing all the fuss are *Africanized* honeybees—imported bees that escaped experimentation in South America and have inexorably made their way north to our cities.

Back to our honey hunters, who collect the honey from the more aggressive *African* honeybee. It is one and the same as the *killer bee* the American press has touted so highly, making the Ndorobo's story even more remarkable.

We encountered two old fellows at a tree with a large beehive that was up the trunk twenty feet and poised for their honey heist. As they saw our vehicle approaching, both of them quickly dismounted and stepped away from the tree, fearing we might be after the honey.

Derrick stopped to ask if they had seen any leopard tracks. As we approached them, Derrick began talking as he pinched a bit of honey from their pails. Meanwhile, I lit a cigarette, and I offered them a smoke. That always seemed to help secure information from the Masai or the Ndorobo.

I noticed the little bow and arrows they were carrying. Each man carried his honey bucket in one hand and his bow and arrows in the other. Their bows were a kind of longbow but only fifteen inches long. Each had a half dozen arrows, twelve to fourteen inches long, the tips of which were coated in a black tar.

I asked Derrick about the tar-like substance on the arrow points. As I reached for one of the arrows, Derrick grabbed my hand and quickly pulled it away.

Maswa—1969

Honey hunters

Honey hunter arrow with tar

Honey hunter smoking

Wandarobo with Derrick and spear

Honey hunter

Honey hunter

Honey hunter

Masai boy

"Don't touch that, Rodger," he warned. "That stuff is poison, and it will kill you quicker than a black mamba!"

Staying well clear of the arrow's tip, I convinced one of the old gents, with Derrick's help translating, to allow me a closer look at his bow and arrows. The shooting system was quite ingenious, a superbly made piece of primitive hunting equipment; I was most impressed.

Having an inquisitive mind and wanting to probe into the matter a bit further, I asked Derrick what the poison was made from and what its effects were on the body after it came into contact with the blood.

Derrick insisted he didn't know, but that he had seen natives test the poison before. One of his former "test subjects" had held out his arm, made a cut above the elbow, and allowed blood to flow freely to his wrist.

He then applied a dab of the poison to the stream of blood near the wrist, and Derrick observed as the blood coagulated when the poison traveled upstream. When it nearly reached the subject's incision, the man quickly wiped the blood from his arm, interrupting the poison's flow.

The subject had told Derrick that when the blood coagulated, the poison was sufficiently potent to kill even the largest of animals.

Derrick reported that he had known of such poison being used by the natives to take down an elephant in a matter of days and that the British had never been able to find an antidote for this poison.

We were making our way through the bush one afternoon and noticed a lone Masai sitting beneath a tree. He appeared to be taking a nap. As we approached him, the sound of our vehicle woke him, and he stood up very quickly. As we drew closer, we could see dried blood on the side of the man's head and face.

Derrick stopped the Rover. He got out and struck up a conversation with the Masai to inquire about any interesting tracks the man might have seen. He didn't provide us with any helpful hints relative to animal signs or tracks, but as to the blood on his face, he said he had an accident.

Apparently, the Masai was quite embarrassed and hesitated to talk about it, but Derrick persisted.

The injured warrior had been making his way through the bush and wanted to have a bit of a nap. Derrick said those guys would take a nap at the drop of a hat; even our boys would do so if they sat still for any length of time.

The spears made by the Masai have a wooden centerpiece and a metal piece at either end. One metal end is rounded and comes to a point. The other metal end is the cutting end and is somewhat flattened out on both sides. It is razor sharp. The rounded end of the spear is for "planting" the weapon in the ground when the warrior stops walking and sits or lies down.

It seems our wounded warrior had stopped for a rest, stuck the rounded end of his spear in the ground by a tree, and sat down under it to take a nap. When he did so, he failed to "anchor" the spear deep enough into the ground for it to remain there until he retrieved it.

As the Masai slept, the spear fell on top of his head and sliced it open six to eight inches and down to the skull. It was healing, but the man would have fared better with a few sutures and a few less flies on the wound.

There were but a few short days remaining on our 1969 safari, and there was still the matter of the elusive leopard. I was beginning to think I might not see him this safari, and I might not get all of the Big Five this trip. I feared I might have to wait till my next safari that I had been planning with Louise. But, that's why they call it hunting. Still, there were two days left.

We came upon a Masai manyatta and stopped so Derrick could speak with the number one headman and inquire into leopard sightings.

After talking with him for some time and forfeiting a few more smokes, the headman told Derrick that one of his tribesmen had seen a fresh kill near the giant boulders not far from where his cattle had grazed days earlier. Derrick decided to have a look because that kind of area with large boulders is prime habitat for baboons, the leopard's favorite meal.

Baboons will move about on large boulders, making it difficult for predators to catch and eat them. They will sit atop a large boulder and groom each other while the older males keep watch. Not only will a leopard kill a baboon, but also lions and other predators find baboons easy targets when they are in the open.

Baboons on large boulder

We covered several square miles before we found leopard tracks that Soko and Derrick agreed were those of a nice-sized male.

There were several large trees near the boulders, and Derrick suggested we hang the carcass of a zebra we had shot earlier that day and take a chance on a leopard visiting for dinner.

We hung the bait in a tree closest to the bottom of a large boulder. Here, we would have an approach to the bait with the wind in our face, and we could build a blind without too much difficulty.

We had some trouble getting the zebra carcass up in the tree on a limb sturdy enough to hold it. With the help of a strong rope and the use of the Rover to do the pulling, we were able to get the bait up and secured to a large limb. Then Soko and Mageli built the blind.

Building a leopard blind is no easy job. Careful consideration must be given to the prevailing winds, since human scent to a leopard is like waving a red flag. The blind must be constructed to ensure its occupants cannot be seen from outside. Any move-ment will alert the leopard, and chances are, you will never even know he was there. A small "plug" for the rifle is left in the front facing the bait.

As we drove back to camp, we planned our approach for the next morning. If the leopard did not come tonight, he might do so the following evening. It was a gamble, but we had no choice except to give it a try, as time was running out.

The next morning, we got an early start to get to the blind at least one hour before daylight. If the leopard came during the night, he would probably still be on the bait at daylight.

Derrick explained that leopard usually feed at night, and just at daylight, they get their last bite before

Building a leopard blind

leaving the bait until the next night. It was agreed that if we got to the bait and the leopard had been there and gone, we would come back early that afternoon and wait him out for his dusk return.

When we arrived at the spot to leave the Rover, we quietly exited and prepared our approach to the blind, two hundred and fifty yards away. It was still very dark with no moon to light up the landscape. A cool, gentle breeze was in our faces as we walked toward the blind. It was so quiet I could hear the others breathing.

I had asked Derrick if I could use his 7 mm Magnum rather than my .458 because it had a six- to nine-power variable scope, whereas my .458 had a less powerful scope and gathered less light.

As we settled down in the blind, we listened for any sounds of the cat eating, but we could not hear any. Minutes passed slowly, and I had plenty of time to get ready for a possible shot, assuming I got the chance. I had fired Derrick's 7 mm Magnum at several small plains animals and felt confident that I wouldn't have a problem.

Sitting in the African bush at night gives one lots of time to reflect. I began to wonder if, after all my waiting, I might not contract a case of "buck fever." I hadn't been nervous with any of the other Big Five, but I hadn't sat in the dark waiting for them, not knowing if or when they would appear.

Certainly, the leopard couldn't shoot back, and I was not that concerned about wounding him and letting him get to me. I guess I was more concerned about missing the critter if he was in the tree on the bait.

The eastern horizon had begun to show signs of light. I struggled to focus on the bait as the configuration of the limbs blocked my view. Had the tom come to the bait? Was he there now? If he was there, was he sleeping or eating? Would he stick around long enough for a shot? I couldn't hear anything nor could I see the bait. A few minutes passed, and Derrick reached over to touch my arm and whispered, "The leopard is lying on the big limb next to the bait."

I then spotted what looked to be a large hump on the elevated tree limb. The barrel of the 7 mm Magnum was lying over the rifle rest that we had earlier constructed for a steady shot.

I put the rifle to my shoulder, looked through the scope, and clearly spied the leopard lying on the tree limb. He wasn't eating—just lying there. Derrick whispered again, "Don't shoot while he's lying down."

I didn't say a word. I was careful not to make a sound as I kept the crosshair on the leopard's shoulder. We watched the cat for five minutes, but he didn't move. Finally, the cat raised his head, stood up, and looked around.

For a fleeting moment, that leopard looked directly at me, staring into my eyes through the dark. I knew I had been busted, that he had seen me, that he would spring from the tree limb and be gone, or worse yet, come for me.

Slowly, the cat began to cat, and he lowered his body to a crouched position with all four legs hugging the limb. His belly almost touched the tree limb as he ate.

The noise was maddening as the leopard tore great chunks of zebra flesh, consuming them with sickening, crunching precision. The cat continued to eat in the crouched position, and Derrick again leaned over.

"If you can get a good shot at the shoulder or chest area," he whispered, "go ahead and take it. He won't be there much longer."

The cat remained crouched, his head pointing away from me. Much of his left side was exposed, and I could see his rump and flicking tail pointing off to my right.

I figured that if I hit him on his left side at the rib cage, the angling bullet would travel up through the chest cavity, through the lungs, and hopefully pierce the heart.

Even if the round missed the heart, it would most certainly break the cat's shoulder or lodge in his neck. Seconds passed like hours, and the wait seemed like an eternity.

I admit, my heart was pumping like a south Texas windmill in a windstorm. In those fleeting seconds, my only thoughts were: *Don't shoot too fast; get a good slow squeeze*. I took a deep breath, let about half of it out, and began the trigger pull. The gun went off, and I heard the bullet strike meat. I knew I had hit that beautiful cat—but where?

The leopard flew from that limb as if knocked down by that same south Texas windstorm. He hit the ground with a thud, and when he did, he hit the ground running. It is true what they say; cats *do* land on their feet—at least this one did. My cat ran twenty feet and collapsed.

"Now that's one dead leopard," Derrick said in his cavalier way.

"I certainly hope so," I nervously replied.

At long last, I had done what I had set out to do—bag the Big Five!

We climbed out of the blind and slowly, with great caution, approached what we hoped was a dead leopard. Upon lighted examination, my bullet had struck the cat at about the fourth rib on his left side. It exited just shy of his right shoulder, as planned.

Soko said, "*Ndio, bwana.*" (Good shot.) Everyone congratulated me as we celebrated and spent some time admiring my leopard.

We took down the bait—that is, what remained of it—loaded the leopard into the back of the truck, and merrily started back to camp.

Thus ended our Maswa hunt. The only thing remaining to do was to return to camp, freshen up, pack, break camp, and start back for Arusha.

When we arrived there late in the day, I had an excellent opportunity to visit with Derrick, Heidi, and their new son, David.

Derrick was quite the proud father, as Heidi had given birth to David while we were in the bush. David is grown now and lives with his family in Salt Lake City, Utah.

Frank and I enjoyed a wonderful evening, recounting the hunt and relishing the modern amenities of Derrick and Heidi's lovely home.

All of the trophies we had collected were packed and shipped to Derrick's headquarters, where they were dried, dipped, and sent by sea freight to Houston, Texas. From there, the trophies were sent to our taxidermists, and some months later, they came to reside where they have been all these years—in Frank's and my trophy rooms—for all to share.

Rodger's leopard—mounted

CHAPTER FOUR

Maswa Revisited

 1971

If the man has the right stuff in him, his will grows stronger and stronger with each exercise of it—and if he has not the right stuff in him, he had better keep clear of dangerous game hunting, or indeed of any other form of sport or work which there is bodily peril.

—Teddy Roosevelt, *Theodore Roosevelt: An Autobiography*, 1913

In March of 1971, Louise and I prepared for a thirty-day safari.

I had booked the safari with Derrick in 1969, when Frank and I had ventured to the Dark Continent. Upon our return, I discovered that the grandeur, the indescribable experience that is Africa, was something that was sorely missed in my life. Indeed, it was hard to get out of my system.

Two years earlier in the Tanzanian bush, when we had thrilled at Neil Armstrong's out-of-this-world feat, I had asked Derrick if he would book a thirty-day safari for my wife and me beginning July 20, 1971, two years from the date of the historic American moon landing. It was a fitting tribute—and anniversary.

"Deal done," Derrick had agreed. And after a torturously long two-year hiatus, I was headed back.

I decided that on this trip, I would ship much of the gear before we left. I had two Air Force footlockers that we filled with all our clothing, as well as everything Louise and I thought we'd need for thirty days in the bush.

I carefully screwed down both footlocker lids and taped them tightly. Then I stacked one atop the other and built a three-quarter-inch plywood container to enclose both for their transatlantic voyage.

I contacted a shipping company in Houston to determine how long it would take to get our shipment to Mombasa, Kenya, to ensure that it would be there before we arrived in July. I took the crate to Houston and sent it on its way before the first of March. The shippers told me that the crate should arrive safe and sound toward the end of May.

Louise and I both were inoculated with all of the necessary shots. I didn't need as many as she did because I had been given some of them on my earlier trip in 1969. And, bless their hearts, our parents had agreed to take care of ten-year-old Michael while we were away.

Louise and I decided to leave early so we could spend time in Europe, seeing the sights and visiting long time friends. By sending our safari goods ahead as we had, we didn't have to lug everything all over Europe.

Our airline tickets and passports were in order, so we were ready to go. As the departure date grew nearer, I began to think about the Super 8 camera I had used on my first safari and how disappointed I was that the experience had passed without sound to accompany the images.

Yes, I had some good film footage, but no, we had spent much of our time hunting, not photographing, and the old Super 8 had no sound capability to record those earlier conversations.

I located a man in Houston, Texas, who had advertised a 16 mm movie camera for sale. I called him and made an appointment to see him.

When I arrived in Houston, I met with the man, whose last name I now cannot recall for the life of me, and I examined his 16 mm movie camera. It appeared to be in good working condition. While Don and I were talking, he explained that he had done work in California as a cameraman and was very interested in my upcoming safari to East Africa.

I asked Don if he had ever been to Africa, and he said that he had not. I asked, "How would you like to go for a couple weeks as my guest?"

Don was shocked. But before he could answer, I said, "If you agree to go the first two weeks in July, I will pay for your airline ticket and all your expenses. You will, of course, be a nonhunting companion to Louise and me if you agree to film the trip for us with your new 16 mm camera—the one that melds sound with imagery. And I will buy all the film. I will not, how-ever, pay you for your services. Consider it a paid vacation." I added that if he agreed, I would still buy the other 16 mm camera I had driven to Houston to consider.

In retrospect, that offer must have taken old Don by surprise. He stood there for several minutes, his mouth agape, his mind, no doubt, doing somersaults and back flips. He finally agreed and accepted my offer.

When I returned to our San Marcos home with my new movie camera, I bought Don a round-trip ticket to Nairobi. We were set to go.

I had no clue how much a nonhunting companion would cost to take on safari, but I really didn't care.

When you stop to think about it, money is only good for one thing—to make your life more comfortable.

The purchase of my new camera and the inclusion of a videographer would allow movies to be taken of our safari with the sound incorporated on the film—in synch. It would also allow Louise and me to be in the picture at the same time. With the second camera, I figured I could capture the action when Don left after the first two weeks.

I practiced with my new toy at home before we departed, and I also bought more than eight thousand feet of color, 16 mm film.

As departure time drew near, Louise and I rechecked our list for all the necessary items we would need on safari. Finally, we agreed that we had everything.

I telephoned Derrick in Africa and told him of our nonhunting, camera companion, whom I had invited along. As always, Derrick was most accommodating and said that wasn't a problem.

We loaded up that last morning in Texas, and after saying our good-byes to our son, Michael, and all four of the grandparents, off we went.

The trip to Europe was wonderful. I'm certain Louise enjoyed it as much as I did. We visited friends in several countries and saw different sights throughout, but this story is not about that European vacation. I couldn't wait to return to Africa, and before I knew it, we were there.

We arrived in Nairobi days prior to the start of our thirty days of heaven on earth—our 1971 safari. The first night, we stayed at the posh New Stanley Hotel in Nairobi. The hotel was uniquely quaint and handsome. The Stanley featured a historic sidewalk café, the Thorn Tree, known far and wide. A legend says that if you sit there for any length of time, you are bound to see someone you know. We did not—so much for legends.

Derrick met us at the New Stanley the next morning to begin the three-hour drive to Arusha. As we got reacquainted, he suggested we sit down for a cup of tea or, better yet, a shot of scotch because he had a bit of bad news for us. For me, that amounted to a nine on the old pucker scale.

Derrick related his good news–bad news. He had checked with customs in Mombasa, where our sea freight had been shipped. The good news: It had arrived. The bad news: There was a longshoremen's strike at the docks, and our stuff could not be moved until the strike was over. There was nothing we could do and no way of knowing when the strike would end.

The least of my worries was the crate sitting on the dock in the weather. I had packed and weather-proofed it to withstand a typhoon. My concern was all our hunting gear and clothes—everything we would need for our safari was in that damned crate. Fortunately, we had our rifles with us, but we would have to hunt in the same street clothes and shoes we wore in Europe—not an enviable proposition.

After Don, the cameraman, joined us, our entourage

made its way to Arusha, where we stayed at Derrick and Heidi's for a much-needed night's sleep. Anxious as I was to get back into the bush, everyone was jet-lagged and concerned with the news that the trunks were sitting on the docks.

The accommodations at Derrick and Heidi's modest dwelling rivaled anything in a 1970s contemporary American home. The furnishings were comfy, and trophies, skins, and photographs hung on the walls. The house was even outfitted with indoor plumbing and electricity. Fancy that. But the key ingredient in their home was the love that filled it.

When we arrived, I noticed there were two new Toyota Land Cruisers in the driveway. I didn't see the old Land Range Rovers Derrick had when my brother and I were there in 1969. Derrick admitted that the Toyota was a "tougher rig" than the Rover—quite an admission for a Brit.

The Cruisers were similarly equipped for the bush as the old Rovers had been—gun racks in the back, grill guards on the front, and a wrap-around railing to keep the boys tucked in the bed of the vehicle.

Mechanically, Derrick admitted he had far less trouble with the new Japanese versions. The old workhorse, Derrick's six-ton truck, was parked outside, ready to carry all of the necessities for a first-class safari.

We planned to leave for Maswa in the morning, but we talked well into the night before turning in. At some point in the conversation, I asked Derrick about his two fine dogs in the yard—a yellow lab and a menacing-looking Doberman. The lab had been given to him by Western movie star Roy Rogers, whom Derrick had taken on safari in East Africa. Fittingly, the dog's name was Roy.

In his good-natured, humorous way, Derrick indicated that Roy Rogers was a pleasant and interesting chap but "not that good a shot."

Another of Derrick's clients was baseball great Stan Musial, whom Derrick said had proved himself to be "a very good shot."

There had been various other clients of note, including an Indian maharajah, who reportedly "was a very pleasant gentleman."

Maswa campsite

Derrick was then, and remains today, an artful storyteller, recounting his many safaris with world-famous personalities.

Morning came, we loaded up, and off we went on another adventurous and exciting expedition.

We took roughly the same route to the Serengeti as we had in 1969—around Lake Manyara, up the slopes of the Ngorongoro Crater, and out onto the plains of the Serengeti into the area known as Maswa.

Derrick had selected a different campsite for this safari than the last. And as ever, it was a beautifully pristine area with tall grass and trees.

We had most of the same equipment as we had used on my last safari, and Derrick provided an

Maswa campsite

additional tent for our cameraman, who seemed delighted with the living arrangements. As before, everyone would be comfortable.

The trip from Arusha to base camp was tiring. We drove it in a single day rather than spending the night at the lodge on the rim of the Ngorongoro Crater as we had in 1969. Knowing my impatience, perhaps Derrick planned it that way. Regardless, I was thrilled to be back in the bush. As many have learned, Africa grows on you.

Asmani cooking

Asmani prepared a tasty dinner for us that night, and as usual, he outdid himself. We had dik-dik steak, potatoes, beans, and, as a matter of course, a nice red wine. Then we were off to sleep. I had not slept that well or that deeply in a very long while.

Louise and I each had an Army-style canvas cot that was most comfortable. The weather was cool, requiring at least one or two blankets in addition to the sheets.

As in 1969, it was winter in East Africa and deliciously cool at night. With canvas, swing-open doors that zipped side to side at the floor and top to bottom, it was not only warm but reasonably quiet. With the tent zipped tightly, we were shielded from a host of tiny African insects should they attempt a visit in the middle of the night. We both slept well.

At the back of our tent, there was a zipped opening that led to a path of wooden planks laid out over the soil, bound for the shower tent.

Each day when we came in from the bush, we changed out of our soiled clothes and dropped everything at the foot of our cots. In the morning, our tent boy, Shibani, picked them up after we left for the bush. While we were gone, he washed and ironed them, and when we returned that night, our cleaned clothes were neatly folded on our cots.

Shibani also kept the canvas floor swept and clean. The sheets on our cots were washed and ironed each day as well. And beside each cot was a small bedside table for our personal goodies and a flashlight. Louise could not have been happier.

Our tent boy also dug our toilets, which were located behind our tent. How he could dig a one-foot, "square" hole in the ground about three feet deep is beyond me, but he did. I never saw the digging implement, but it must have been a square shovel.

Finally, there was a potty stool placed over the hole for our toilet.

Derrick's tent was identical to ours. Likewise, our PH had his own shower tent and potty tent.

The camp was kept neat and clean, and the dining tent was no exception. There was a nice dining table covered with a white linen tablecloth and set with crystal and silver service. Keep in mind, this was in the wild African bush. Our refrigerator was propane gas operated, and as a consequence, we always had an ample supply of ice for our toasties.

The setting described above will not be found on one of today's safaris. Such tented safaris are gone forever but not forgotten.

Asmani was a real heavyweight chef who could have held his own in any French five-star restaurant. Every time we sat down to a meal, there was no doubt Asmani's feast would delight us. And every bit of his fine cuisine was prepared on an open fire or in a bed of coals.

Louise showed him how to make Texas-style cornbread, and he baked it several times on safari without another word from my wife. Asmani, as well as all of Derrick's crew, catered to our whims.

Derrick was proud of his safaris. He especially took pride in the little things that made for a pleasant journey. And he was proud of his crew and their abilities to do their jobs. On safari, if we asked for anything, he made certain we had it. An example was my first breakfast.

I had just sat down in the dining tent when Derrick entered. "What would you like for breakfast, Rodger?" he asked.

"Eggs and toast—perhaps a little meat," I replied. Derrick asked how I wanted my eggs prepared, and I said, "Sunny-side up, please."

In minutes, Tibiri, our mess boy, entered the tent carrying a white towel draped over his arm with my breakfast. I was about to cut into my eggs when Derrick stopped me with a shout, "Asmani!"

The cook came running in, whereupon Derrick grabbed my plate and handed it to him. A few words were spoken in Swahili, and Asmani left with my breakfast.

I asked Derrick what was wrong, and he replied calmly, "On my safaris, if you want your eggs sunny-side up, that's the way you will have them. Your yoke was broken." I said it didn't matter and that I was about to cut them up anyway. From then on, I ordered my eggs scrambled.

That first day before sunrise, I awoke to the sound of an elephant screaming in the distant bush. Birds began to chirp as if to alert everyone that a new day had begun. Each morning of every day, the bush came alive outside our tent with the exciting sounds of East African wildlife.

As a matter of course, as I lay there waiting for Shibani to come in with our morning tea, I contemplated what the day would bring. I knew that whatever it might be, this time Louise was in the picture, and the trip would be more exciting and pleasurable than my last safari. At long last I would share the grandeur and the spectacle that is Africa with my dear wife.

I recall the conversations I had with Louise upon returning from my first safari and how I had broken the news to her about booking another safari with Derrick—this time, for the two of us.

I recall her excitement and how much she had looked forward to the trip. As excited as she was, however, Louise insisted that there were two animals she would most definitely *not* shoot—the lion and the zebra.

The lion, she had explained, loses all its natural beauty when it's dead, and she was just not into shooting horses. I had not pressed the issue, and I said, "No problem, honey. I already have my lion, and I will gladly shoot your 'horse' for you because I want the zebra skin for a rug." Problem solved.

After our tea, we joined Don in the dining tent for breakfast. Derrick arrived and took our orders. After eating my sunny-side-up egg, we gathered our gear and headed out for a day in the bush.

It was a gorgeous morning. The sun was bright and the sky azure. We loaded into one of the Land Cruisers and started out into the world of the East African bush. Derrick drove (right-hand drive), Louise was in the cab in the center, and I was on the left-window side.

Soko and Mwatumbuki, our trackers, were standing in the back, and Don was riding in the back seat. In 1969, Soko and Mageli had been our gun bearers and trackers.

In 1971 Mageli was no longer with Derrick and had been replaced with Mwatumbuki. That was just fine with me because, as it turned out, Mwatumbuki proved to be a much better tracker and gun bearer.

I had my .458 Model 70 Winchester and, for Louise, my .375 Model 70 Winchester H&H Magnum for buffalo, elephant, eland, and greater kudu. The loads I brought for the .375 were 300-grain solids for the elephant and 270-grain soft-nose bullets for buffalo, eland, and greater kudu.

Louise's eland

I was certain the weapons and rounds would do the job. I had the same loads for my .458 as before, which had proved more than adequate.

Looking back now, it has been thirty-five years since that brilliant experience, and it's very difficult to gather all of the events in order.

Louise's impala

My recollection is that since I wanted Louise to experience all that I had experienced two years before, I wanted her to take all of the plains game I had taken, plus some other species I had not taken earlier.

We came upon topi; kongoni; Grant's, Peter's, and Robert's gazelle, and Louise made some remarkable shots on those plains antelope. When we came across a herd of zebra, I would shoot. We were each allowed two zebra on this safari. She also shot an excellent impala and a Coke's hartebeest. The Peter's gazelle Louise shot was as good as Derrick had ever seen.

She made an outstanding shot on her eland. He was out about a hundred yards and walking slowly. That .375 has more than a slight bump to the shoulder by way of recoil, and it will punish you if you don't seat the butt of the stock well against the shoulder.

She was aware of the recoil because she had fired it several times at home before departing for Africa. Derrick told her to go ahead and take the shot even though he was walking slowly. She led him a little as she was taught to do and fired that powerful rifle. The .375 made a convincing statement when she pulled that trigger; not only could you hear it, but Louise could feel it as well.

Louise's lesser kudu

When she shot, I could hear the bullet hit meat and knew that she had made a good shot. The eland went down and never moved. As we approached the eland, I could see that she had made a perfect shot into the shoulder, penetrating the animal's heart.

I asked our cameraman to capture our time in the bush that morning; I was hopeful that he had gotten some good shots. I had asked that whenever possible, he include Louise and me in the picture, and Derrick too. I suspected he was getting some great footage because he was really going through the film.

It was getting close to lunch, and we were beginning to work up an appetite. Although the Land Cruiser was not a really rough-riding machine, it was not the softest in the world, either. Bouncing over the rough

Louise's Robert's gazelle

African countryside helped whet our appetites.

Derrick selected a good spot to break for lunch beneath a big, shady acacia tree. We spotted baboons climbing and sitting on the giant boulders just to the rear of the big tree under which we had lunch.

Baboons are very curious animals. Some of the larger males can deliver a nasty bite with their gigantic canines. They are not terribly aggressive but will stand their ground if threatened.

During lunch, we saw several female warthogs with young shoats running across the grass fifty yards away. We hadn't spooked them, and Derrick suggested that a predator must have frightened them.

When warthogs run, they hold their tails straight up

Louise's roan

said that the larger bulls are generally located at the fringe of the herd as it moves but that sometimes the big animals will trail toward the rear of the herd.

The buffalo were aware of our presence as we drew closer in the vehicles, and Derrick pointed out two nice bulls at the back. We kept moving alongside in an attempt to separate the herd and scatter them.

The Cruiser bounced along steadily as we gave chase. We were trying to keep up with the two larger bulls as they made their way across the grassy plain.

Derrick explained that most of the time when you trailed alongside a herd, many would veer away to one side, thinning the ranks. Sometimes, a small group would stop and watch the vehicle as it moved beside them.

A group of eight or ten animals had fallen back. We could see the two larger bulls that Derrick had spotted in this smaller group. Derrick moved the Cruiser out toward the head of the bunch and stopped.

Soko knew that if we were able to get a shot, he was to get Louise's .375 and my .458 out of the rack so Louise could take the shot.

Derrick and I had already had this conversation about Louise shooting her buffalo. I had asked him if I could back her up with my .458 when she shot it. He no longer questioned my ability to handle a rifle, saying, "You may not be a Western movie star, Rodger, but you are a very good shot. Go ahead. Back her up."

Buffalo herd

We got closer to the bulls, stopped, and got out of the Cruiser. Louise and I walked out in front, and the larger of the two bulls stopped. Derrick was immediately behind me with his .470 at the ready. Lest we forget, the Cape buffalo is an intelligent and dangerous animal.

The small group of buffs was moving back and forth, creating a good bit of dust. Louise and I were about thirty to forty yards from the largest bull.

He stood broadside to us as Louise raised her rifle. I never said a word but had my .458 to my shoulder with a round in the chamber ready to squeeze off if, after Louise shot, the buffalo charged us.

Louise fired and hit that rascal perfectly. He stumbled

and almost went down but instead turned his head away from us and tried to run toward the rest of the herd. Louise chambered a second round about the time the bull turned and fired a second time. That shot hit him in the rump.

I never fired a shot; it wasn't necessary. This was Louise's animal, and backup wasn't needed. My wife had done her job brilliantly!

The rest of the herd was now out of sight as Louise's buffalo stumbled into thick bush and collapsed. We stood quietly in our tracks, and we remained rooted for twenty-five to thirty seconds, listening.

There was no further movement from the buffalo. We heard nothing, so we started for the thicket where he fell. Derrick carefully approached the bush solo with his .470.

Buffalo are dangerous animals and should be considered so until they have stopped breathing and their heart has stopped pumping blood.

As we approached the spot where we thought he was, Derrick stopped and shouted, "That's a dead mbogo. Come on over."

As Louise and I drew closer, I could see that the bull had fallen roughly five feet from what this old Texas boy calls a ravine or a ditch. Had he made it another five feet, it would have been tough getting him out.

Louise was ecstatic. She had clearly shot a Cape buffalo that would qualify for the record books. The buffalo measured forty-seven inches, four inches better than my Cape buffalo in 1969. The animal weighed in the vicinity of eighteen hundred pounds, and he had a very heavy boss. Louise now had the first of her Big Five, lacking only the elephant and leopard (she would not shoot a lion, and there were no black rhino permits).

After many congratulations and handshakes, we had a round of cold Lone Star beer. I have had many ask how on earth I was able to secure Lone Star beer, a Texas-brewed beverage, in the wilds of East Africa.

The truth is, I took a half dozen empties with me to Africa and filled them with the local brew during the hunt. After all these years, the true story has now come to light!

Louise's 47 1/2" cape buffalo

When asked by folks viewing our trophy room, "Hey, Rodger, is that a Lone Star beer in your hand?" I have replied, "Yes, sir, my PH can provide you with whatever you want when you're on one of his safaris!"

We called it a day after Louise shot her buffalo, and we victoriously made our way back to camp that afternoon, tired but pleased.

We had traveled a good distance from camp on the buffalo hunt, traveling past a Masai manyatta. As we came to it once more, Derrick asked if we would like to stop and meet the chief—see a bit of the African culture. We agreed, and he pulled up to the front of the manyatta.

Louise's Buffalo

It was daylight, and there were no cattle to be seen. Derrick explained that the cattle were out and about grazing, with the younger children tending to them. The women and very small children were no doubt gathering wood for their fires or doing other daily chores.

The number one man was home, and he invited us into the manyatta. Masai build their huts in a circle. They move their cattle in with them at night, and they close the entranceway—not to keep their cattle in but to keep the predators out.

Upon entering a manyatta, the chief's hut is first on the right. The remainder of the huts are built counterclockwise around the circle of the inside fenced area, and a tribe member's status is determined by the proximity of his hut to the chief's dwelling.

Stuck in the ground outside one of the huts was a Masai warrior's spear. I asked Derrick if a warrior lived there. "No," he replied. The spear was there to indicate that the chief had given that warrior one of his wives for the night.

The wealth of a given Masai tribe is determined by the size of its cattle herd. Generally speaking, the greater the wealth, the more wives the chief has, and each wife is afforded a different hut.

After we pulled away from the manyatta, we continued scouting for animals on the way back to camp. As we moved along, with Soko and Mwatumbuki standing in the back looking for game, I spotted a man standing alone in the tall grass about one hundred and fifty yards out.

I asked Derrick to stop the Cruiser, and I explained that I had seen a man standing there; I pointed to the spot. Derrick said he had not seen anyone and that I must have seen an animal. He yelled up to Soko and Mwatumbuki and asked if they had seen a man there. Neither had.

I repeated to Derrick that a man had been standing there, but as I spoke, he had squatted down in the grass, as if to hide. I was emphatic. I explained to Derrick that although he was the animal expert, I knew a man when I saw one, and what I had seen was definitely a man.

"Okay," Derrick agreed. "Let's have a look."

As we approached the spot, we considered the possibility that I might have seen a poacher. We had seen several abandoned campsites, but we never had seen a poacher, at least not that we could confirm. We drew closer to the spot, and I told Derrick to stop. It was right about there—I pointed—at that spot that I had seen what I knew to be a man standing in the tall grass. We all got out and cautiously looked around.

Soko was the first to speak. *"Bwana, pole, pole."* (Sir, slowly, slowly, over here.)

We joined Soko, and there was indeed a very old Masai woman squatting in a tiny, dugout, earthen ditch. The woman was totally alone.

She had a small fire going, and there were several old tin cans about that she obviously had been cooking with. And there was a small pile of what appeared to be some wild berry or pod of some kind that she had been eating. Derrick couldn't identify the plant, and Soko was unfamiliar with it.

As we stood there, the "little old lady from Maswa," as we later named her, crawled back into her home and began speaking with Derrick. She was obviously not pleased with our presence.

Masai woman in bush

Soko walked around the area and called out to Derrick. Soko motioned to Derrick to join him where he was standing. The spot where Soko stood was roughly the place where I thought I had seen a man standing and squatting. When I got there, Soko was moving away with a look of disgust etched on his face.

The little old lady had been using the area for her potty, and there were the remains of partially digested yellow pods she had eaten. Derrick explained that the boys could handle all of the blood and guts associated with the hunt, as well as a host of unsavory items, but this was beyond their tolerance level.

Louise asked Derrick what the old woman might be doing out in the bush alone, so far away from everything. When the Masai get old and are deemed useless, he explained, they simply wander off to die. Large predators hasten the inevitable for the lucky few; the other outcasts die from hunger and exposure. We loaded up and regretfully left the old woman as we found her, to her god and her world.

After we got back to camp, we sat down for our usual

Masai woman in bush

toasty and enjoyed the evening waiting for Asmani's dinner to be served. We discussed our trunk that had been held up on the docks in Mombasa because of the strike and wondered if we would be able to collect our possessions when we returned to Arusha. We also talked about the animals we had taken and what a thrilling experience it had been.

Louise and I went to our tent to get out of our dirty clothes and take a wonderfully hot shower. Then we went to the dining room and had a delicious wine with another of Asmani's scrumptious dinners.

Early the next morning, we started back to Derrick's home in Arusha. En route, we saw giraffe, Thomson's gazelle, impala, warthogs, cheetah, and most of the plains game. That's really what an African safari is all about. You wander through the bush, learning about the various plants and animals as you go. You experience the thrill and the beauty of everything around you.

We arrived at Derrick's to find Heidi and their son, David, doing well. There was also a big surprise. Our long-awaited crate with all our hunting gear had arrived. It was like Christmas. How on earth had we gotten along without everything that we had shipped to Mombasa?

Opening the crates and clearing the contents through customs had been no problem. But we did have one amusing experience with the customs officer.

Derrick had told me before we came on safari that I would not be allowed to bring the two .45 caliber, single-action Colt revolvers into the country. Tanzania would not allow handguns to be brought in, but I was determined to try.

When the customs officer got to my revolvers, he had a puzzled look on his face. He did speak a bit of English and asked, "What's this?"

I quickly took one of the handguns, held it, and laughed, "Oh, Roy Rogers, boom, boom."

To which he replied, "Oh, yes, Roy Rogers—cowboy movies—I know movies," and set the revolvers aside.

The only other item in the crates that got his attention was the large bag of lemon drops Louise packed for tasty treats. The officer said, "Oh, no, bwana—not allowed."

I quizzed Derrick about the lemon drops, and he said that we could not bring candy into the country without paying a duty because they made candy in Tanzania.

I said, "Fine," and handed the lemon drops to the officer.

I asked Derrick to tell the man that I brought the lemon drops from Texas as a gift for him.

He replied, "*Asante, bwana,*" (Swahili for "thank you, sir") and stuck the lemon drops in his briefcase. We were good to go.

CHAPTER FIVE

Rungwa

 1971

If you have enough money, you can still shoot a white rhino today. I said shoot, not hunt. One will be driven into a large enclosure for you by official personnel. You may then walk up to the condemned beast and kill him, nice and neat, no walking, no risks. You can spend the air trip back home thinking up a nice, scary story of how you stopped his charge from mere inches when your white hunter lost his nerve and you had to save his life. The presence of a recently shot white rhino on anybody's wall is, to me, tantamount to mounting a red banner inscribed "FRAUD."

—Peter Hathaway Capstick, *Death in the Long Grass*, 1977

The next morning, we were off to a new hunting area, one that I had never seen before. It was located roughly five hundred miles south of Arusha, in an altogether different type of terrain.

The area was known as the Rungwa Game Reserve. It was a rough area with many trees, including the baobab tree of the silk-cotton family, sometimes referred to as the "upside-down tree." Baobab trees have an edible fruit that resembles a gourd.

There were large stones and many different types of thorn bushes scattered throughout the area as well. Although it was winter and the dry season, there were rivers running through the Rungwa with pockets of water remaining. The Rungwa is a massive hunting area encompassing many hundreds of square miles.

The area was noted for large elephant, sable antelope, leopard, greater kudu, roan antelope, topi, hartebeest, and many poisonous or otherwise dangerous snakes—python, black and green mamba, and cobra.

It took two days' travel to reach the planned campsite, so we got an early start from Arusha. We drove one of the very few improved roads as far as it would take us; then we traversed dirt tracks for most of the first day.

We had gone about three-fourths of the way when we headed east through bush so heavy we had to hack our way through.

Giant fig tree at camp in Rungwa

Soko under candelabra tree

Fig tree trunk

Baobab at sunset

When we returned from the Serengeti, we had left our guest cameraman in Arusha for his return trip home. Don had done his job, although when the film was developed, we found that the audio input on his camera had failed to work. Bummer. After all that, there was no sound. Oh well, life's a bitch sometimes.

Don was able to get some good film, but in retrospect, I think the film I shot with my 16 mm camera was better. Between the two of us, however, we did come away with some excellent African footage.

We made a fly camp (a temporary overnight camp) to stay the first night and planned for an early start the next morning, as the boys had some serious cutting to do with their machetes to clear the way for the vehicles.

Derrick has a son and daughter by his first wife, who died years before. His daughter, Val, was a teen at that time—about eighteen years old—and she wanted to go with us to the Rungwa, assuming it was okay with Louise and me. We said that, of course, it was. Besides, she would be great company for Louise, who had been surrounded by men from the start of our adventure.

Early the next morning, Derrick was in the lead Toyota with several boys out in front of us, chopping away with their pangas. Soko was in charge, and since he had been there many times before with Derrick, he knew where he was going and how to get there. What a guy he was!

Suddenly, one of the boys ran back to our vehicle

and informed Derrick that they had found a large puff adder where the boys were clearing brush. We jumped out and made our way there.

The boys were standing back from an indentation in the ground. The spot was about six feet in diameter and was covered with dark brown leaves.

They kept pointing down at something, but I couldn't see the object of their excitement—obviously some sort of snake. Derrick looked around and pointed. "There, Rodger. There he is, right there."

A few seconds passed as my eyes and brain connected the dots. Finally, I could make the object out. It was a very well-camouflaged snake, perhaps three to four inches in diameter. I had been told puff

adders were deadly, but I had never come across one before. Now I had, coiled ominously before me—only inches away.

"Go get your Colt revolver, Rodger," Derrick urged, "and kill the bastard." Before anyone had a chance to react, I grabbed Soko's machete and, with several quick chops, cut that puff adder into pieces. The boys were aghast. Derrick was more than slightly irritated.

This was not some act of bravado on my part—simply instinctual. I had run across many rattlesnakes in Texas, and this was how we handled such reptilian threats in the Lone Star State. Deal done.

I could tell without him saying, Derrick was not a

happy camper. In retrospect, perhaps it was not the best thing to do—hack a dangerous snake to pieces with a machete. The better part of valor would have been to shoot the rascal, but I didn't want the noise to frighten off any animals.

Derrick insisted that discharging the revolver would not have frightened the animals. I suppose in many ways I still considered myself a bite-proof twenty-one-year-old. No matter; the snake was dead, and I was fine.

We made it to our intended destination at mid-afternoon, and it turned out to be a great place for a campsite. Immediately, the boys began setting up camp.

The entire camp fit beneath one fig tree—the tree was that massive. Before or since, I have not seen such an enormous fig tree, the trunk of which had to have been six to eight feet in diameter.

Camp was situated close to the Isawa River bed. Giant baobab trees surrounded us, and the place was quite the subtropical paradise.

The boys did a fine job preparing a comfortable camp for us. And while Louise was getting our clothes together in the tent, I cleaned the firearms and organized the ammunition.

While cleaning the rifles, I wondered about our chances of bagging a big bull elephant for Louise. She also needed her leopard, a nice greater kudu, and perhaps a fine sable.

It was too late in the day to start out into the bush, so we rested up before gathering around the campfire for our first toasty. Conversation that night was stimulating, as it always was, with Derrick delivering his safari stories of interesting clients and exciting hunting adventures. His stories are unbelievably humorous, and I have absolutely no doubt of their veracity. Without a doubt, Derrick is my oldest and best friend.

The next morning, we were up early and on our journey. We made our way eastward along the northern bank of the Isawa River in search of game. Louise scored a very nice topi that first morning, and we saw many other creatures we had not seen before.

My wife also brought down a very nice roan antelope. We drove along the river for quite some time before Derrick suggested we try our luck fishing. The Isawa held catfish, and one of Asmani's specialties happened to be fried catfish. That river is very wide and deep during the rainy season, and although it was nearly dry now, there yet remained pockets of standing water.

As we were preparing to fish, all at once, a female greater kudu was spotted with a nice male behind her, standing in the bush staring at us. Soko handed me the .375 as I got out of the Cruiser.

The female moved off, but the male remained motionless. Derrick leaned over the left side of the vehicle and softly whispered, "Rodger, that's a really good greater kudu. Take him!"

The kudu bull was only thirty-five yards out, hiding in thick brush. I could see a bit of his shoulder, and I thought I could squeeze a round into the kudu's shoulder without a rest for the rifle. I squeezed off a round, and I heard the bullet hit.

Before I could speak, Derrick said, "You hit him! He's down." We were elated.

Catfishing near hippo pond

As we approached the downed kudu, I could see that he was, in fact, a very nice trophy. I wished Louise had taken him, but the thorny bushes were very thick, obscuring her shot. In any event, there would be another for her to take. We skinned him out and put him in the back of the vehicle.

Derrick remembered a bend in the river, where the

water would probably be deep enough for some fishing before we had our lunch.

Before reaching the fishing spot, Derrick dropped Soko off at the riverbed and told him to make his way up the river bottom to see if he could find any fresh elephant tracks. Derrick told him to go up about two miles and meet us back at the river, where we were to fish and have lunch.

Derrick indicated that it was about a mile down-stream to his "honey hole." We had only two rods to fish with, but that was enough.

We drove for about twenty-five minutes along the river, having to make our own tracks. When we got halfway there, Derrick stopped and pointed outside his window. "Look, there. Four or five kudu."

Fishing for catfish near hippo pond

I saw several kudu moving through the bush, and they did not appear spooked. Derrick said this would be Louise's kudu, assuming one merited taking.

Louise and Derrick got out of the Cruiser, secured her rifle, and started off into the bush. Val and I stayed put. After about twenty minutes, we heard a shot. It sounded as if the bullet hit meat. Val and I got out and starting walking in the direction of the shot, but I didn't take my rifle. I did have one of the .45 Colt revolvers, just in case.

We hadn't walked far when we came upon Louise and Derrick. Both had big smiles on their faces. Louise had the rifle slung over her shoulder, leading the way.

"Well," I asked, "did you get a good one?"

Lunch and fishing near hippo pond

Derrick smiled and said, "I think it will measure better than yours."

Derrick's report made my day. I had taken the first kudu, and I really wanted Louise to get hers. There is an interesting story associated with my wife's shot. As they say, position *is* everything.

Louise explained that she and Derrick had slipped through the thick brush a good way before Derrick turned and spoke.

"There are two standing close together," he reported, "and the one on the right is the better of the two."

As Louise's story goes, at the time, Derrick and Louise were kneeling down, peering over a small bush for a look at the kudu. Derrick informed Louise that

Hippo pond

the kudu on the right was the one she wanted, but Louise could only see one animal.

Derrick repeated, "There are two; yours is the one on the right."

Again, Louise said she could only see one. The conversation was repeated yet again, Derrick saying there were two kudu, and Louise insisting she could only see one.

Finally, Derrick squatted down beside Louise. With his head lowered to hers, he discovered that he too could only see the one animal. A small bush was in the way.

Derrick is a good bit taller than Louise. He moved her to her right so she was somewhat elevated.

Finally, she could see the good kudu as well. Derrick reported Louise then made an excellent shot. Position is everything.

As we got up to the kudu, it was obvious that Louise had made a clean, accurate kill shot. As usual, I was very happy and very proud of her.

We turned back to the vehicle, and Derrick worked his way around the thick bush so he could drive closer to the downed kudu. The greater kudu I had shot two hours earlier was still in the back of the Cruiser. Before we loaded Louise's animal, we decided to take photos and movies of both her kudu and mine.

We unloaded my kudu, which had already been skinned and put both heads together while capturing what Derrick described as a rare event—getting two very fine greater kudu within a few hours of each other.

Louise and I were overjoyed to have taken two excellent greater kudu on the same safari and on the same day. And Derrick was absolutely correct—Louise had taken a kudu that was larger than mine.

Mwatumbuki tended Louise's kudu while we had our lunch, after which we went fishing. We caught and kept eight to ten nice-sized catfish for the evening meal.

I must say, both Soko and Mwatumbuki were more than capable of tracking their favorite animals.

Greater kudu

Theirs were incredible skills. Mwatumbuki preferred the elephant, and Soko's game of choice was the greater kudu.

I had been busy with the new 16 mm camera, and I was getting reasonably proficient with it, if I do say so myself. As I was running off some of the eight or nine thousand feet of film I had brought along, I noticed Soko coming our way, walking in the sandy river bottom about a thousand yards away. During my filmfest with the kudu, Derrick told us that Soko would be delighted that Louise had bagged her greater kudu.

With Soko approaching, I called to tell Louise he was coming. "Run up and tell Soko about your greater kudu," I urged my wife, "and I'll capture the action—and Soko's reaction—on film."

She started off in his direction, and I caught it all on film. As she got close, she shouted to him that she had killed a greater kudu. Soko stopped in his tracks and immediately stuck out his arm to shake hands with Louise, obviously very happy for her. When they returned to the Cruiser, Soko had to have a look-see at her animal. When he did, he was all smiles.

Derrick came over with the catfish and asked Soko if he had seen any tracks. Soko said that he found no fresh tracks, so we loaded up and headed back to camp.

The sun was setting on the East African horizon as we drove up to camp. As we disembarked, there was an awesome sunset with a very old, magnificent baobab tree silhouetted against the orange sky. With the setting sun, it was getting cool, and Louise and

Sunset in the Rungwa

I headed for our tent to get out of our dirty clothes and have another delightfully hot shower.

To shower in our African shower tent, you had to do like the sailors do in the Navy—conserve water. First, you got completely wet by pulling the rope and releasing the water. Then you turned off the water and soaped up before repeating the process and washing off. If there was water left, you simply enjoyed the hot water longer.

After showering, Louise and I headed for the campfire and our first toasty of the day. The boys always had the fire stoked and the toasties ready after a day in the bush.

The next day, we headed back into the bush wondering what we might see. We had not come across a good elephant yet, and the Rungwa was one of the best of the East African locales for big elephants.

Making our way through the bush that day, we found an oryx and a waterbuck, both of which Louise shot. There were vast numbers of oryx and waterbuck in the area.

Around midday, we were heading through an area covered with large baobab trees and deep gullies. This was a splendid place for leopard, and since it was time for Louise to get her chance at old *chui* (Swahili for "leopard"), Derrick decided to hang bait and see if we could entice a big cat.

We had the oryx carcass Louise had taken, so we had perfect leopard bait for that night. And after driving

around, we spotted the perfect thorn tree from which to hang it.

We stopped the Cruiser and hoisted up the carcass. We tied it to a large limb twenty feet off the ground and selected a good spot for Soko and Mwatumbuki to build a blind.

The approach to the blind was excellent, and the prevailing wind would be just right for that afternoon's hunt. If one didn't come that night, we would try again in the morning.

It was still early, so Derrick decided to scout for fresh elephant tracks, if there were any to be found. We started off along the edge of the Isawa's dry riverbed in search of any sign. We brought along an extra skinner that morning to help out, since the back of the Cruiser was loading up with carcasses each day.

Derrick knew that Soko and Mwatumbuki were reasonably familiar with the river along that stretch, as they had been there with him before. Derrick stopped the Cruiser and told Mwatumbuki and Mathoka, the extra skinning hand, to get out and walk up the river to a point about two miles away to search for elephant. When they reached a certain point, they were to come out of the riverbed and wait for us.

We drove along the riverbed in the Cruiser, passed the point where Mwatumbuki and Mathoka were to meet up with us, and continued up the river's edge to a point two or three miles away. There, we dropped off Soko and the other skinner with instructions to come back and meet at the designated rendezvous point with Mwatumbuki and Mathoka.

We then turned around and started back to the meeting place. It took us about two hours to accomplish this. When we reached the midway point, we stopped and waited.

By then it was close to lunchtime, so we gathered up our goodies that had been packed for us before daylight and began to eat lunch. We waited for an hour or more for Mwatumbuki and Mathoka to show, but there was no sign of either.

A bit later, Soko and the other skinner came in from the other direction. Derrick thought this odd, as Mwatumbuki and Mathoka should have been back first. He passed it off, saying they probably got sleepy and stopped for a nap.

Derrick cranked up the Toyota, and we started back down to find our missing trackers. We hadn't gone far when we saw Mathoka running at top speed toward us, carrying his little panga as he ran.

Derrick quickly stopped the vehicle. "Something's wrong," he said.

Mathoka was out of breath when he got to us, and it took him a few seconds to gather himself. Then he began to tell Derrick what had happened. Mathoka reported that Mwatumbuki had been gored by a buffalo.

"Damn," Derrick swore.

"Did he say Mwatumbuki is dead?" I asked.

"Hell," Derrick said, "He doesn't know, and I don't either."

Mathoka jumped in the back of the Cruiser, and we raced pell-mell back for Mwatumbuki.

I admit, Derrick made good time getting back down that tract. There we were, five hundred miles from any medical facility. And it had taken us two hard days' driving to get to our current location. On the way, I could only imagine what we would do if Mwatumbuki was dead.

I began feverishly getting my camera out, thinking, I suppose, that I was some news reporter from a television station going to cover an accident. Louise had a fit. "Don't you dare take any pictures when we get there," she said. I quietly put the camera away and held on.

As we approached the spot where Mwatumbuki lay, the first thing I noticed was blood running from the man's nose and mouth. Mathoka had dragged Mwatumbuki up to our track, and the injured man was sitting down, leaning against a tree. We got out and hurried to Mwatumbuki's side.

After Derrick had administered a shot of morphine, we learned by bits and drabs what had happened. (Note: A licensed professional hunter can legally carry morphine in the bush for just such an occasion.)

Mwatumbuki and Mathoka had discovered the tracks of an elephant going through the river bottom. They followed the tracks into some very thick underbrush by the riverbank, when all at once, they spooked a large bull Cape buffalo that had been lying in the tall grass.

No doubt, the buff spooked our trackers as well. I would guess it scared the digested breakfast out of both of them.

Mathoka told us that he ran as fast as he could back toward the river, but Mwatumbuki had attempted to climb a tree. The problem was, the tree was only six inches in diameter.

The buffalo charged the tree Mwatumbuki had climbed and knocked the tree to the ground with Mwatumbuki hanging on.

With nothing more to do, Mwatumbuki lay flat on the ground, face down, as the buffalo made another pass at him, goring him in the back and running away. When the dust cleared, Mathoka came back to help Mwatumbuki and ended up hauling him up to the tree by the track where he now lay.

Derrick did everything he could for his man, cleaning the wound and slinging his right arm in a position that wasn't as painful. We gingerly loaded Mwatumbuki into the vehicle and slowly started back to camp.

It took us an hour to get back. By that time, the morphine had taken effect, and Mwatumbuki was not in as much pain.

On the way to camp, Derrick and I had discussed our options. I asked if he thought we should attempt to fly Mwatumbuki out for medical attention in Aru-

sha or Nairobi and if it would be possible to clear a spot for an airplane bush landing to evacuate the injured man.

Derrick said we could but that it would cost about six hundred dollars. I told Derrick it was not a matter of cost; I would handle that. No one wanted Mwatumbuki to die.

Derrick suggested we wait until we got back to camp and see how extensive the injuries were and how Mwatumbuki was doing. After we had a chance to speak with him, we would decide upon a course of action.

On the way back, we came near the leopard bait and decided to wait until early the next morning, depending on Mwatumbuki's condition, in hopes a leopard had discovered it and eaten.

At camp, Derrick administered antibiotics to the injured tracker. Fortunately, I had brought some with us, just in case.

Mwatumbuki was a bit doped up but was in remarkably good spirits. He even apologized for his carelessness for letting the buffalo gore him. We assured our tracker that it had been an unavoidable accident, that it was certainly not his fault, and that he should rest.

As Mwatumbuki rested, Derrick came over to me and said, "Let's you and I take Soko and go back there, see if we can track that buffalo, and shoot the bastard."

I immediately agreed, "Let's do it!"

We loaded up—me with the .458, Derrick with his .470, and Soko with his skill, stamina, and jungle smarts.

We made good time getting back to the place where Mwatumbuki met his match, and Soko had no difficulty locating the buffalo's tracks. Soko was in the lead, then Derrick with his .470, and me with my .458.

There was little to no conversation as we moved cautiously, following the buff's tracks. Derrick commented that the tracks and the path the animal was running didn't make sense. Soko was curious as well.

The bull would run, then walk for no apparent reason. He would travel through thick bush to get to a point in a clearing. The reverse was more natural; it would have been easier for the buffalo to run through the clearing rather than through the thick bush.

I asked if buffalo were susceptible to rabies or anything to cause such erratic behavior. Derrick said he didn't know but that it was possible.

We had tracked the buff for a very long way when, all at once, Soko stopped. He said nothing, simply pointing his finger straight ahead.

Derrick and I saw the buffalo at the same time. I was told to take the shot if I thought I could hit him at that distance. The buffalo was seventy to seventy-five yards directly in front of us. Soko squatted down to the left, in front of me. I didn't say a word as I shouldered my .458.

As I readied myself for the shot, the scope turned black. Soko had been squatting down when I brought my rifle up. In the interim, he moved a bit to his right and stood up.

Now, his head filled my scope picture. Soko's head was directly in line with the muzzle of my rifle.

I raised my rifle with a jerk. Derrick saw this and immediately fired twice with his .470. I heard the second shot strike flesh. The buffalo rolled over and came off the ground running. Fortunately, he ran away from us.

Had I squeezed off a round, I would have blown Soko's head off. Neither Derrick nor I ever said a word to Soko.

We walked to where the buffalo had been when Derrick fired. We found a tiny bit of blood but no buffalo. We followed the blood until the trail ran out, but we never saw that buffalo again.

We made our way back to the Cruiser and returned to camp. By the time we arrived, it was nearly dark.

To our amazement, Mwatumbuki was standing with Louise. Val stood nearby, waiting for us to get back to camp. They asked what had happened as we sat down to our toasty.

As the flames licked at an ebony sky, we related our story. Naturally, Mwatumbuki was disappointed we didn't get his buff. So were we.

Had the buffalo been an old bull, kicked out from the

Toasties by the campfire

herd? Had he been snared and wounded by poachers and seeking revenge? Or had he just reacted instinctively, attempting to protect himself? We will never know.

Derrick had a long conversation with Mwatumbuki. He had left the decision to him as to whether he wanted us to fly a plane in for him or not. The tough Mwatumbuki said he was feeling better, although he knew he had been broken up a good bit. His scapula and clavicle were very sore to the touch, and he said his rib cage was very sore as well. Still, he wanted to stay on with us because we had only a few days left to hunt. Derrick agreed.

After dinner that evening, Derrick said we would start very early in the morning to see if Louise had a leopard in the tree, so we all turned in early that night.

The next morning, we got away very early and arrived at the place we were going to leave the Cruiser for the approach to the blind. We got there in plenty of time to make an approach without being seen or smelled by the leopard, assuming one was on the bait.

After daylight, we saw that the leopard was not there, but one had been on the bait during the night. Derrick said we would make another attempt later that day for an evening shot. Hopefully, he would come back.

We went on about the business of hunting, and after

we had been through the bush for a good long while, we came upon a sable antelope.

The Rungwa was an excellent area for sable. Derrick had commented during one of our evening campfire chats that it was most unusual we had not yet seen one.

We drove to an area where Derrick said he had always seen sable, always in the early mornings. We drove slowly, viewing many animals—impala and Thomson's gazelle. Then we saw waterbuck and a very nice sable.

Louise took that sable with a single attempt, and we were delighted that she had made such a good shot. Her sable measured thirty-six inches—a very nice trophy indeed for an East African specimen.

That afternoon, we loaded up and made our way to the leopard blind in hopes one would drop by for an evening feast. We settled down into the blind and began our wait.

Just before dark, he appeared and climbed the tree like a cat will do, with no effort at all. Leopards are amazing climbers. Earlier, Derrick had told Louise to let the leopard settle down and start eating before she shot.

It wasn't long before Louise fired, and she brought down her leopard with one, well-placed shot. By that time, it was almost totally dark. Derrick preceded Louise with his .470, just in case. Fortunately, the big cat had expired. Louise had made a terrific shot on a very nice leopard.

We had a pleasant evening our last night in the Rungwa, and we hated leaving the next morning. Our safari had been perfect. The weather had been delightful, and all of the animals beautiful and plentiful. We had not seen elephant in the area, but we knew they were there. Large as they are, elephant can be terribly elusive creatures. Derrick reminded us that we were scheduled back in about fifteen months for a twenty-one-day safari to Mkomazi, and he reminded us how great an area it was for elephant.

As we were leaving the campsite, Derrick suggested we carry our rifles, as we might still see game on our way out of the Rungwa. The boys were not far behind in the truck with all our gear and our trophies.

Louise's leopard

We had been looking for an excellent sable antelope. Louise had shot a nice mature sable, but the older the animal, the darker his hide and hair and the longer his spiral horns. As we left, ahead of us and to our right stood a troop of five mature sables.

Derrick brought the vehicle to a halt, and we both got out with our rifles. We began to walk toward the area where the sables had stopped.

As we cautiously approached the troop, we both spotted the bull that looked to be the largest. I drew down on his shoulder and fired. The troop scattered, all except one: the sable I had hit. He was a magnificent trophy.

Rodger's trophy sable antelope

Derrick was very excited. He said he had never seen a sable in East Africa with horns so long. He immediately went back to the Cruiser and got the measuring tape. My sable measured forty-seven and a half inches. Derrick recalled hearing that the largest sable taken in Tanzania was thirty-eight inches. If his memory served him, my animal might well merit the Shaw and Hunter Trophy for 1971.

I immediately asked, "What's the Shaw and Hunter Trophy?"

Derrick explained. In the early to mid-1950s, the East African Professional Hunters Association created the trophy to be awarded to the professional hunter and client jointly responsible for taking the best animal in East Africa that year. The animal could be a dik-dik or an elephant. The award was discontinued in the mid-1970s.

As it turned out, our sable was the winner that year. That was the first time Derrick had won the award but, as you will soon learn, not his last.

Louise, Rodger, and Heidi with Shaw and Hunter Trophy

CHAPTER SIX

Mkomazi

 1972

In after-years there shall come forever to [the hunter's] mind the memory of the end-less prairies shimmering in the bright sun; of vast snow-clad wastes lying desolate under gray skies; of the melancholy marches, of the rush of mighty rivers; of the breath of the evergreen forest in summer; of the crooning of ice-armored pines at the touch of winter.

—Teddy Roosevelt, *The Wilderness Hunter*, 1893

ctober 1972 came slowly but surely, and Louise and I were off on another safari with Derrick Dunn in East Africa for twenty-one gloarious days. When we arrived in Nairobi, Derrick collected us at the Thorn Tree in the New Stanley Hotel. But he was not alone.

Accompanying him were two wonderful people who had just completed their safari on the Serengeti. They were Paul and Joany Deutz.

Paul and Joany had been on safari with Derrick before and were very good friends of the Dunns. Louise and I found them to be a delightful couple, and we have since become good friends.

Paul took down a Cape buffalo in the Maswa, where Louise and I had hunted the year before. That bull turned out to be the number one, all-time largest Cape buffalo killed in Africa.

The bull measured 59 5/16". That is more than remarkable—almost unbelievable—but a certifiable truth. To this day, Paul's bull remains the world record and Derrick's second Shaw and Hunter Trophy.

Another prestigious East African professional hunter named Syd Downey won the award twice, but Derrick won it twice in consecutive years. No other hunter has ever accomplished that feat.

We left Paul and Joany at the hotel, and Louise, Derrick, and I loaded up in the Land Cruiser and headed for the Tanzania-Kenya border crossing and on to Arusha.

On the way, Derrick said he had little doubt that Paul's buffalo would win the Shaw and Hunter Trophy, and we were all very pleased. I remember thinking to myself that I had hunted in Maswa twice and never seen that big buffalo, but he must have been out there when I was there. I just didn't see him. If it wasn't me that bagged that trophy buff, I'm glad Paul got him hunting with Derrick.

The next morning, we would leave for a new area. It was reasonably close to Longido, where I hunted in 1969 and bagged the Big Five. The place was located on the southeastern slope of Kilimanjaro.

Mkomazi is not quite as vast as the Rungwa or Maswa, but it is known for its many elephants. Derrick said there was much of the same, smaller game that we had taken in the other areas, but we were not interested in duplicating that which we had already killed. However, we did need two more zebra rugs and several additional animals for our trophy room at home.

We arrived in Arusha at Derrick's home and greeted Heidi and David. The lad was now three and a half years old and growing up too fast, like most little guys. To see and know him now, it's hard to imagine he was ever a little boy. David is an American citizen, married, and lives in Salt Lake City, Utah, with his wife and family.

Mkomazi isn't as far from Arusha as Maswa or the Rungwa.

We drove there in only four hours. Our campsite was yet another beautiful area, although quite different from the other areas we had hunted. We were excited because en route, Derrick had told us of the many herds of elephant there. Our camp was located near the Tsavo National Park in Kenya, east of the majestic Mount Kilimanjaro, towering 19,340 feet.

After camp had been set up, we relaxed a bit and discussed our plans for the next day. We checked the area to see what fresh tracks of larger elephant had been made. We spent most of that first day driving about the area. When we spotted tracks that were interesting, we would move to higher ground and glass the area in search of the herd that had laid down those tracks. Sometimes it would behoove us to head over and catch up near the herd, then walk with rifles, ready to investigate closer.

If you have hunted Africa or watched films of an elephant stalk, you may recall the cloth bags that trackers carry. Such sacks are filled with burned wood ash, and the trackers shake these bags to determine wind direction.

As I have recorded earlier, you had better stay downwind of the herd. It doesn't matter whether they're bulls or cows, you do not want elephants to detect your scent. Even if you think you have a strong wind in your face, that wind often swirls, distributing your scent. Elephants will become very excited if they suspect a man is nearby. Either they move away or they come after you, depending on the elephant.

Bull elephants often distance themselves from the herd, especially if they are older and larger. However, herds with very small, young calves and cows can be just as dangerous as a bull that has become aggravated.

Each herd generally has an older cow that serves as the matriarch. She rules the family. When she moves away, the herd moves away with her. On most occasions, when a human is present, the matriarch will move out in front of the herd to stand off the intruder. She may make short bursts forward, raising her trunk in defiance. She may scream and flap her gigantic ears back and forth, attempting to ward off the interloper.

I had always thought that flapping of ears was a prelude to an elephant charge. Derrick corrected me, saying that was not the case. But when an elephant puts both ears flat against its body, rolls its trunk under, and puts its head down, watch out! That elephant is about to charge. Elephants are much faster than you might think, and your chances of outrunning one are not good.

As we know now, there is one and only one spot to place a bullet into an animal to increase the odds of making a clean kill. This is the only ethical and safe way to hunt, and it may prevent the animal from running away and dying.

An elephant is no exception. Many people talk about a head shot on an elephant, but the area on the side of an elephant's head is not a very large target. A great many elephants have been tracked for miles and never stop after an attempted brain shot didn't reach its target. The only sure kill shot is a shoulder shot.

We had approached a small herd of cows and calves as we were moving along in the Cruiser when the matriarch stopped to look us over.

Apparently, she didn't want our vehicle anywhere near her herd. There were several very small calves, some of which Derrick said did not look more than a few months old. The worst time to approach an elephant herd is when there are young calves present. The herd's alpha female does not want or need any assistance in caring for her herd, and any person or animal that comes near is considered a threat.

Accordingly, the matriarch made threatening gestures with her ears and trunk and moved forward a few steps, raking up much dust and shaking her head violently. Translated, that meant "please move on." We did so without hesitation.

Tracking elephant

Mkomazi—1972

Throughout the day, we looked over four or five smaller herds before we came upon one that Derrick hoped might have a large bull lurking close by.

Louise stalking elephant

We stopped the Cruiser, got out, and readied our gear for a walk. I wanted Louise to have the first chance at a bull since I had mine in 1969.

Soko grabbed the .375 with a magazine filled with four 300-grain solids that were ready to chamber one at a time for the elephant. Derrick led with Soko by his side, the bag of ash gently shaking up and down as he walked. Louise was directly behind Derrick, and I was behind Louise.

I left my .458 in the Cruiser, as Derrick had the .470 Rigby to back up my wife, if necessary.

I carried the camera, and Mwatumbuki was behind me. This stout fellow had healed remarkably well in the fifteen months since his terrible experience with that mad buffalo in the Rungwa.

We made it to within seventy-five yards of the herd, but there was no bull to be seen anywhere. Derrick figured there had been a bull passing through, but he must have moved on as we approached.

At that instant, the herd matriarch must have detected our scent. The old girl spotted us and did not like what she saw. Contrary to conventional wisdom, an elephant does have adequate eyesight to see what danger may be around. She roared a deafening scream and threw up her head, flapped her ears, and took a few steps toward us.

Derrick raised his .470 and got off a single round directly into the forehead of that cow. The dust flew. I couldn't hear the bullet impact because we were so damned close. It took me by complete surprise. I hadn't expected Derrick to hammer that elephant.

That stopped her in her tracks. The matriarch shook her head, turned, and moved away from us at a fast walking pace. It got real quiet.

I asked our PH, "Did you shoot that cow in the forehead?"

"I sure did. And it stopped her," he said.

Derrick later explained that the round went into the vast bony sinus area of the cow's skull. If anything, it only gave the old girl a headache.

Derrick went on to add that there were many elephants with spent bullets in their sinus cavities, and it did them no permanent harm—only stunned them temporarily.

Sitting on the side of a small hilltop, we continued our search for a bull, and it wasn't long before we glassed two good ones. They were walking away at a steady pace below, about a half mile away.

Derrick said we would have to hurry to get in the Cruiser and move down and around them in an effort to cut the bulls off before they got out of the valley. So off we went, down and around, dodging rocks, logs, trees, and whatever was in our way to get ahead of those two bulls.

We pulled up to a spot where Derrick thought we were well ahead of the pair and, if they had not changed course, gauged they would appear in a clearing ahead. The wind was right, and in about fifteen minutes, we saw the two heading right up the open area to our right.

Derrick positioned Louise so she could get a good shot at roughly forty yards away as the two passed by. That wife of mine was some trooper for a city girl who had never hunted before she met me.

There she stood in the middle of East Africa with a .375 Winchester Magnum against her shoulder, waiting for a four-ton dangerous animal to approach to within a short distance. Then she would stand up to the challenge that thousands upon thousands of

Louise ready to shoot

hunters dream of but never get to experience.

I've got to say, when she fired that .375, I saw the bullet hit that gigantic creature, and it started down, I was very proud of her. She chambered and fired a second shot into the bull before he hit the ground.

Derrick said that her first shot entered the animal's heart, and, in his opinion, the bull died instantly. Louise and I were very pleased about that.

It was then that the work began. It takes quite some time to chop out a set of ivories. Of course, the boys had done it many times before. Still, it's a job. The boys skinned out the ears, tail, and feet for trophy mounting.

As best Derrick could judge, each ivory weighed in the neighborhood of eighty pounds. That's a fine elephant in anyone's book. Hundred pounders were few and very far between because most of the very large bulls had been poached and sold on the black market. Derrick said that if we could get one eighty pounds or better, he would be pleased. Louise had, and she had a very nice trophy.

Derrick decided that he should head back to camp and collect Hamisi, our chief skinner, and another boy to help work on Louise's elephant. It was getting on in the day, and Derrick wanted to get the skins off before nightfall for fear predators would ravage them. He left for camp, saying he would be back in about an hour. Soko and Mwatumbuki stayed with Louise and me at the carcass.

Louise's Elephant

Derrick wasn't gone more than fifteen minutes when Soko shouted, *"Tembo, bwana! Tembo!"* and pointed at the rear of Louise's elephant.

Louise and I had been sitting on the bull's side, and when we turned to look, we saw a cow elephant coming for us.

Soko and Mwatumbuki ran as fast as they could away from the scene. Louise and I didn't need further instruction or coaxing.

Louise's elephant with David, Heidi, and Derrick

I told Louise, "Follow me!" and grabbed the .375 that had been propped against the dead elephant. To say that we left quickly would be a profound understatement.

As Louise and I ran through the bush, we could hear

the cow behind us, crushing trees as she ran. When I looked over my shoulder, I could see the elephant twenty-five yards behind, on my heels. Louise was nowhere to be seen.

Running for my life, I pulled back the bolt on the .375 and chambered one of two rounds remaining. When I reached the next clearing, I decided I would stop, and if that cow was still there, I'd shoot her between the eyes above the sinus cavity.

I ran a bit farther, reached the spot, and looked back for the cow. When I did, she veered away and disappeared into the bush.

The adrenaline was racing through my system. What a hoot! There I was, a middle-aged, country lawyer standing alone in the thick bush of East Africa. I couldn't hear anything except my own heart beating. I didn't know where my wife had run, and my two gun bearers had deserted the area—and us.

I started walking slowly back in the direction of the downed elephant to locate Louise. As I moved along, I yelled, "Louise, Louise!"

After a few minutes, I heard a faint voice ahead and to my right, yelling out, "Rodger, Rodger! I'm over here!" I had found my wife.

We made it back to the downed elephant and found it just as we left it. Soko and Mwatumbuki were nowhere to be seen. We decided to wait until Derrick returned with a cold Lone Star beer.

"Ndio, bwana," (Swahili for "Yes, sir,") a cold beer would taste pretty good, even if it had not been brewed in Texas.

Derrick finally arrived with Hamisi, the extra skinner, and Soko and Mwatumbuki in the back of the Cruiser. Derrick said he had picked up the two missing men on their way back to camp. Soko had relayed our "elephant skirmish" to Derrick.

Derrick belatedly warned us that we should have crawled beneath the dead bull's underside. "Then," he said, "the cow would have gone away."

Easy for him to say, I thought. I added that I had always heard that when an elephant was down, the other elephants would try to help the downed elephant to its feet.

Derrick said that was true, assuming the downed elephant was still alive; if it was not, the others would have nothing to do with it. So much for twenty-twenty hindsight.

Derrick decided we should return to camp and take Soko. He could bring back the other Cruiser and collect Mwatumbuki, the skinners, and the elephant parts. That way, we would have more time at the evening campfire with our toasties. Sounded like a grand idea to Louise and me. We both could use a "splash" in the shower.

The fire was roaring when we returned, and we were ready to relax and have that scotch we had been dreaming of all the way back to camp.

As usual, the boys had everything ready. There was a stiff breeze that evening, and when it blew like that, the boys erected poles with canvas stretched between them to shelter us and protect the fire.

During evenings around the fire, we enjoyed sitting and watching the eyes of hyenas that had gathered "outside" in hopes of finding bits of food. They seldom found any because it was not a good idea to leave food around for predators. The hyenas put on a show for us with their lonesome calls.

Then again, we might hear an elephant scream in the distance, and the night would come alive with the sounds of the African wilderness. It was awesome.

That night, we had an opportunity to discuss the next day's hunt and the animals on which we would concentrate. We needed a lesser kudu for Louise, and we still needed another zebra to fill our license. We were also short a roan antelope for Louise, and I did want to get my elephant in the Mkomazi. I had taken my first elephant in 1969 in Longido, but my license also included one for this trip.

I had several hundred feet of film left, and I wanted to put it to good use. Derrick suggested we try another area of Mkomazi that might afford us a shot at the animals we desired and was a little different country than we had previously seen. Reportedly, there were more *kopjes* (Swahili for "hills") there. Perhaps we might come upon another bull elephant making his way toward the Kenyan border and the Tsavo National Park. Derrick suggested we get up early and put in a full day. We agreed and called it a day.

During the night, we had what Derrick said was an unusual light rain for that time of year. It was not a heavy rain but one that caused us to use four-wheel drive off and on through the morning. By late morning, the sun had dried things fairly well. It was deliciously cool and a bit cloudy.

Soko and Mwatumbuki had been alerted that we wanted the lesser kudu and roan antelope, as well as another bull elephant, if possible.

The rain had made it a bit less difficult to spot tracks, allowing Soko and Mwatumbuki to see smaller tracks from the back of the Cruiser.

This area was covered in kopjes, between which the valleys ran in every direction. The slopes and valleys were spotted with animals. Giraffe, ostrich, stein-buck, and other smaller game could easily be seen from the tops of the hills. We knew it would only be a matter of time before we saw the lesser kudu and roan that Louise needed to fill her license.

As we made our way to the top of another small hill, Soko tapped on the top of the Cruiser and informed us that there were roan on the side of the hill. He said that several looked like trophy animals.

Louise and Derrick got out and made their way to

a small boulder, where they stood for a minute or two and looked them over. They came back to the vehicle and reported that there weren't any trophies in the bunch. We continued our search.

We moved in and out of the valleys till we neared the Kenyan border. There was nothing indicating where the border was exactly, but Derrick knew because he had been there many times. He commented that the vehicle track made by the Kenyan and Tanzanian game wardens was very close, paralleling the border on either side.

Tsavo National Park in Kenya is a wildlife sanctuary. The animals seemed to know that fact well, and they frequently used the area as a haven.

As we moved east along the border, we saw two zebra on the Tanzanian side, running in the direction we were headed. They were about a hundred yards out, moving along at a clip, wasting no time.

Derrick was certain the zebra were heading for the park. We were moving at fifteen to twenty miles per hour, and the zebra were staying up with us as we moved along.

According to Derrick, the one in the rear was the stallion. If I wanted to take him, Derrick said he would keep up with the animals until I told him to stop. I should watch for a clearing in front of the zebra, he said, and when it looked like I had sufficient time to get out and take a running shot, I should tell him, and he would slam on the brakes. He suggested I use the bonnet (hood) of the vehicle for a rest.

Dust plumes billowed from the escaping zebra. I saw a clearing and told Derrick to stop, so he slammed on the brakes—more dust.

I grabbed my rifle and jumped out. I put my arm across the hood of the Cruiser but found it hot, so I quickly removed my arm and shouldered the rifle. I would have to take an off hand shot.

The zebra picked up speed, and it would be a very tough shot. The first zebra came into my sight picture. I could see the stallion one zebra-length behind the mare. I quickly calculated and led the stallion at a distance of ten feet.

My scope's crosshair was on the mare's rump, so the stallion's neck and shoulder should claim the bullet. I followed the mare in the scope, and when the crosshair was on her tail, I fired.

The target was a long way off. I heard the bullet clap and lowered the rifle, then looked up to see what had happened.

The stallion tripped, as if over a small barricade and he rolled over his neck. The mare shifted and was gone.

The next sound I heard was Soko. "*Bwana, bwana!* Good shot!"

Derrick got out of the Cruiser, his head shaking side to side. "What a lucky shot!"

I smiled and extended my hand to shake his. "Guess I violated your rule, Derrick. This one was not a shoulder shot. I think I actually broke the stallion's neck." Derrick agreed.

He stepped off the shot distance and calculated that it had been very close to one hundred and thirty yards. I have to admit, there was a bit of luck involved with that zebra shot, although the neck was my target.

We ate lunch while the boys skinned my zebra, and we discussed our plans after eating. Derrick suggested we continue along the border track and see what might be moving around.

After the boys finished skinning the stallion, we moved out along the track for a mile or more. Derrick decided to turn off the border track and make our way down through the valleys again to look for Louise's roan and see if we couldn't find another bull elephant. Earlier, we had seen the tracks of a smaller herd.

The wind had picked up. That can be good or bad for elephant, depending on which way the herd is moving.

Yellow necks were plentiful along the track, so as we drove slowly along, Derrick stopped. He, Louise, and I grabbed our shotguns and began flushing birds. Francolin, as they are also known, are tender, tasty birds about the size of small chickens. They are delicious.

Derrick said the discharge of shotguns wouldn't disturb our hunting because the small hills were so plentiful, they would muffle the sound in the area. We gathered several plump birds for camp meat and went on our way. The sun was bright, and there were no clouds in the sky—simply a beautiful day.

It's terribly exciting to drive around, not knowing what you will see as you top a hill or get to the other side of a thicket.

You may see a pride of lions, a cheetah lying down napping, or warthogs running with their tails straight in the air. There may be a giraffe with its neck stuck in a tree, browsing for tender foliage. Or you may see a Thomson's gazelle giving birth. Such things are a part of the real adventure. This is safari, not just the killing of animals.

As we made our way around the hills, we were surprised to see small herds of elephant down in a large open area, perhaps a quarter of a mile away. They were walking slowly toward the Kenyan border and the park.

We stopped, and Derrick and Soko looked them over carefully with binoculars. Derrick said that there were two bulls following the herd, but he could not get a good look at their tusks because of the brush. He said that we would work our way closer, but we would have to hurry.

We moved to the spot Derrick wanted to reach before the herd passed by, and he stopped the vehicle. We

Stalking elephant.

got out and stalked to where we could view the herd as it passed by.

Soko had Derrick's .470; I had my .458 with solids—just in case.

The herd stopped and began to browse on acacia trees. They did not appear to be in any hurry.

The wind was shifting, and it was difficult to tell which way it would blow at any given time. As mentioned before, the wind is one of the most critical aspects of an elephant stalk. True, their eyesight is not the best in the world, but their hearing and sense of smell are superior.

Unless you have experienced an elephant hunt, there's no way to explain the stimulation one's body goes through. You know that you are, or may be, in a position of danger, but that is natural under the circumstances. An elephant can mangle or crush you with his trunk, and his feet are lethal, massive, jackhammer weapons. A mature bull easily weighs from four to four and a half tons.

The bulls that had been following our herd had veered off to the right but were walking somewhat faster than when we first began. We were concerned they might catch up and mingle with the herd, making it more difficult to get a clean shot at whichever animal we determined was a worthy trophy.

Derrick whispered that we should move up and to our left to have a better look at the two bulls. We did just that.

After moving ten or fifteen yards, we were able to see both bulls as they cleared the thick brush. The bull's tusks were about the same length, and neither was broken. Both were reasonably symmetrical, but one had tusks that appeared to be larger in diameter. Derrick estimated that the one with the more symmetrical tusks might weigh in the neighborhood of seventy-five pounds.

As we stood waiting, the bulls were moving to our left. The wind was still quite brisk but coming from the northeast, blowing in a southwesterly direction.

The bulls were walking due north, as best we could tell. This was fine, provided they did not change course.

The bull that I chose to shoot was in front of the other. If I shot him, that could present a problem.

Should I knock him down, there was no telling which way the other elephant would run. We certainly did not want to have to shoot a second elephant if he came toward us. But that was a chance we would have to take.

Derrick touched my shoulder and whispered, "We are going to get a little closer." We moved over to our right, a few feet, around a lower, thick bush, then stopped.

"When he comes by the larger tree," he said, pointing to a tree to my right, "Shoot him."

I didn't make a sound. I had already chambered a round, so I was ready.

As the elephant came around the tree, he turned a bit, but his left side was toward me. I could get a shot into the elephant's left shoulder, but it would have to enter at an angle. I couldn't see the second elephant.

I fired into the bull's shoulder. He stumbled as I slammed in a second round. I fired again at the same spot, and he started down. I fired a third time into his left side, and the bull collapsed

I never saw which way the trailing elephant moved. Derrick said that he moved off to the right and went out of sight. We stood there for nearly a minute, watching the downed elephant, making sure he didn't get up.

Derrick congratulated me on my shooting. We closed the forty-five-foot span and approached my elephant. Derrick walked back for the Cruiser and returned in twenty minutes.

As Louise fetched us a cold Lone Star, I retrieved my camera from the Cruiser and continued to record our safari.

Then, a very interesting thing happened. While filming the elephant and its processing prior to taking it back to camp, I noticed Africa's little dung beetles at work. They are interesting, industrious little creatures.

When the elephant hit the ground and expired, he had excrement on his backside—evidence of an

Rodger's Mkomazi elephant

earlier meal. Dung beetles immediately (and quite literally) flew into action.

Dung beetles are about an inch in diameter. They gather dung so they can lay their eggs inside a rolled ball of manure. When the young dung beetles hatch, they subsist on the excrement.

Adult dung beetles rummage about in animal dung, continuously rolling the partially digested stuff into a ball about the size of a softball. When the parent beetles have gathered enough material to roll into a ball, they push the ball along until they find a suitable place to bury it.

The ball of dung is damp, and as it is rolled by the tiny dung beetles, the ball gathers soil and grows

Dung beetle

larger and larger. As they move along, now and then a dung beetle climbs atop the dung ball for a better look. Then he climbs down and continues rolling the ball toward its final resting place.

Dung beetles then kick the dirt from beneath the ball, and it slowly descends into the ground until it is totally covered. I found this most fascinating to watch and film.

After gathering our gear, we started back to camp. Our safari was over. We had but a day or two remaining in Arusha before Louise and I were to fly home to Texas. Many thoughts ran through my head as we approached camp that afternoon. Louise and I had had the experience of a lifetime.

I realized then there would never be any way to duplicate such an adventure. We bagged all of the trophies we came for, and they would remain with us as testament to our trip for the rest of our lives, safe and sound in our trophy room.

Many guests have viewed that trophy room in our Texas home and asked about our African experiences, but I have never been able to adequately explain to them what it really was like on safari.

It is my hope that this book, photos, and DVD will do that.

There are a few events that occur in our lives over which we have no control. One is where we are born. I have no doubt that my luck of the draw was to be born in the United States, to live in a free country.

God bless the United States.

God bless the Second Amendment.

KWA HERI

(Swahili for "Good-bye and good night!")

Zimmerman's trophy room, Waco, Texas

Goodbye "Kilimanjaro"

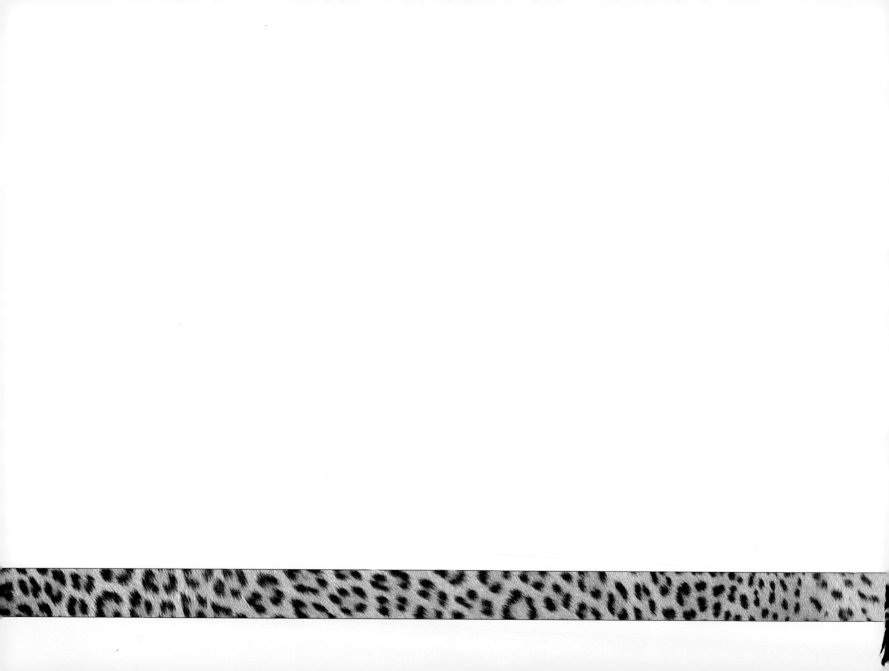